55

40¢

The Challenge of
ISRAEL'S FAITH

By

G. ERNEST WRIGHT

THE UNIVERSITY OF CHICAGO PRESS

Chicago · Illinois

THE UNIVERSITY OF CHICAGO PRESS, CHICAGO 37
Cambridge University Press, London, N.W. 1, England
The University of Toronto Press, Toronto 5, Canada

63-4290

To

E. D. W.

AND THE HOME WHICH HAS MADE THESE
LINES POSSIBLE

FOREWORD

MISUNDERSTANDING and distortion of the religion of Israel are certainly prevalent in our time. Few are the writers who have presented the theological propositions of that religion in a forthright and positive manner, claiming for them an eternal validity and a decisive importance for the Christian of this day. The current fashion of thought has regarded the Old Testament as a monument of antiquity, interesting to the historian, the literary critic, and the archeologist but of little serious value for the life and thought of the modern Christian. Our approach to it has been by means of an overconfident "historicism," wherein it is assumed that, once we are able to trace the accurate, detailed history of the linguistics and institutions of the Hebrew people in their proper life-situation, our task is finished. In reality, however, it has scarcely begun. Those of us who are Christian theists are still faced with the fundamental question: What is the relevance of the prophetic "Thus saith the Lord" for our day?

My concern in these pages, therefore, is not with the history of Israelite religion but rather with the central propositions of Israelite faith. The chief and all absorbing interest of the historians and prophets was not with themselves or with the great leaders of their past, but with God. It is he who is the chief character of the Old Testament, not Abraham, Moses, David, or Isaiah. The *theology* of the Old Testament, therefore, ought to be our major interest, to which all other branches of our study are contributory. To be sure, the prophets (with whose thought we are mainly to concern ourselves) were not systematic theologians in the sense that they present us with a

v

systematized statement of their doctrine. Nevertheless, they were in full and conscious possession of a doctrine, one which interpreted the crises of life in terms of God's wrath and his grace. Further, we must admit that it is impossible to lump all periods of Hebrew history together and treat their religious conceptions in a systematic way without a genetic approach. Yet the bulk of the literature of the Old Testament was either written or edited between the tenth and fifth centuries B.C., and it is dominated by a striking uniformity in point of view. To magnify the differences in conception or emphasis out of all proportion, as is so frequently done, is to be guilty of an understandable, but nevertheless curious, myopia.

Some readers may find my approach confusing and may feel that I am presenting a thesis which needs far more support from the Old Testament itself and from contemporary scholarly literature than I give in the text or in an occasional footnote. The fact is, however, that I am less concerned with the presentation of a thesis than with the attempt to describe just what Israelite religious leaders believed. One reason for such confusion, if it arises, may be the lack of familiarity with a positive treatment of Old Testament theology. Not merely is this subject neglected in modern biblical teaching; it is almost entirely forgotten. The present generation of English-speaking scholars has not produced a single basic text in this field. The best English work is still that of A. B. Davidson (*The Theology of the Old Testament* [1904]), a book which the author was unable to complete before his death, the published volume being inadequately edited from his notes and now out of date in many respects. German scholars have moved far beyond the American and British worlds in this area, as may be seen from the perusal of such excellent works as Eichrodt, *Theologie des Alten Testaments* (1933); Köhler, *Theologie des Alten Testaments*

(1936); Buber, *Das Kommende* (1932); Hempel, *Gott und Mensch im Alten Testament* (2d ed., 1936); and the studies of Israelite conceptions behind New Testament words in Kittel, *Theologisches Wörterbuch zum Neuen Testament* (1933——); etc. Those who are familiar with these works will not find here an approach which is basically new or unsupported.

As far as I know, my approach is neither liberal nor conservative. Such terms have outlived much of their usefulness. It is quite true that there are extremists who disregard Old Testament theology completely and remain content with "historicism." It is also true that there are those who go to the Bible with a certain system of dogma which they proceed to find there by the use of texts without context, in complete disregard of the findings of modern research. We need to approach the Scripture with a point of view which transcends such extremes; and in chapter i the attempt will be made to outline the essentials of this approach. In none of the chapters is there a complete treatment of all aspects of the subject presented. Instead, I have made a selection of certain important topics to illustrate how fundamental the primary articles of Israel's faith are to modern Christian thought and life.

I am greatly indebted to my colleague, Professor Joseph Haroutunian, for the many hours which he spent on the manuscript. He has helped me with numerous insights into biblical and contemporary points of view, and especially with more adequate means of expressing what I wanted to say. Certainly, any value which my material possessed has been greatly enhanced by his generous interest. I am also indebted to Professors J. L. Adams, R. A. Bowman, R. W. Frank, A. A. Hays, and W. A. Irwin, who have read all or part of the manuscript and have made a number of helpful suggestions.

G. E. W.

McCormick Theological Seminary
December 15, 1943

TABLE OF CONTENTS

I. "Thus Saith the Lord": The Eternal in the Temporal . . 1

II. "Choose You This Day": The Meaning of History . . . 17

III. "Obey My Voice": A Chapter on Terminology 36

IV. "For I Am Thy God": The Living and Anthropomorphic God 48

V. "Ye Shall Be My People": The Covenanted Community . 68

VI. "Behold, the Days Come": The Outcome of History . . 82

Postscript 98

Index 107

CHAPTER I

"THUS SAITH THE LORD": THE ETERNAL
IN THE TEMPORAL

IT WAS some twenty-seven hundred years ago that the prophet Isaiah lived in Jerusalem. Yet Christians and Jews in this day still believe that his message in some measure is authoritative because it is more than a word of man; it is also a word of God. If he were standing among us today, he undoubtedly would speak to us in this vein:

Ah, sinful people in your fevered, heaving world! Why think you can turn your backs upon your Maker and Ruler without suffering and bleeding for it? A horse knows its owner, and a dog its master, but you do not know, nor do you possess the good sense of your animals. You are a brood of evil-doers; and in selfish arrogance do you imagine that you can live as though you were God himself? Nations are raping nations; man is at the throat of man. Multitudes are calling evil good and good evil, putting darkness for light and light for darkness; but you have not regarded the word of the Lord, nor have you considered his working in this world. Has this present chaos no lesson for you? You say to those who can see it: "See not!" and to those who can prophesy about it: "Prophesy unto us smooth things that are easy to hear!"

Hear the word of the Lord unto you: What unto me is the multitude of your religious services? Your many churches, your expensive organizations, your gold and your silver and your brass; your exclusive attention to the even operation of your churches, your desire to be nothing more than "nice" people, the lightness with which you regard your mission and com-mission—these things and many more have become offensive to the Al-mighty. Therefore, he'll not hear you when you piously and pleasantly bow yourselves down in prayer. Wash you and make you clean. Cease to do evil; learn to do well. Seek justice; relieve the oppressed. Let us reason this matter: if your sins be as scarlet, can they become white as snow? If they be red like crimson, can they become as wool?

Many of you draw near to God with your mouth, and with your lips you honor him; but your hearts are far from him, and reverence of him is but a

1

commandment of men that someone has taught you. Therefore are the countries of this world desolate, and cities devoured with fire! For upon this world has descended the judgment and the wrath of God. "Ho, Berlin, you rod of my anger," saith the Lord; "the staff of my indignation. The sins of this my people have reached my nostrils, and the stench of them is unbearable." Lying, dishonesty, pride, rebellion, and idolatry are on every hand. The punishment is sure—behold the present darkness and distress! For upon us is a day, a day of the Lord of Hosts, upon everyone who is proud and haughty, upon everyone who is great in his own eyes, upon every high tower and upon every fortified area. And the loftiness of man shall be bowed down, and the haughtiness of man shall be brought low, and the Lord of Hosts shall be exalted!

But the Lord does not punish merely to quench an anger. It is clear that you on this earth will not learn except as you suffer and enter the door of hope through the valley of tribulation. Yet the Lord will not keep his anger forever; neither will he always chide. If you who now stumble in darkness see the great light, if you repent and say: "Come, let us go up into the mountain of the Lord that we may walk in his paths and that he may teach us of his ways"—then, indeed, will a great day dawn, a day ushered in by the Lord God of Hosts among the remnant of the righteous. Then it will be that the Lord will judge between the nations, decide concerning the peoples; and they shall beat their swords into plowshares and their spears into pruning hooks to the end that nation shall not lift up sword against nation, nor shall they learn war anymore.

Take heed, therefore, and be quiet. Neither let your heart be faint. For in repenting and rest shall you be saved; in quietness and confidence shall be your strength. Though the Lord give you the bread of adversity and the water of affliction, your ears shall hear a word behind you saying: "this is the way; walk in it." And thine eyes shall see that the work of righteousness shall be peace, and the effect of righteousness, quietness and confidence forever.

It was in this manner that Isaiah spoke to his people in the eighth century B.C., and so he would speak to us: "This is the way; walk in it; for the Lord hath spoken. How do you know that the Lord hath spoken? Look about you and observe what has happened because of your sinful rebellion! 'Behold,' saith the Lord, 'heaven and earth are witness: I have nourished and brought up children and they have rebelled against me. Ah, sinful people, laden with iniquity, why will you continue to be stricken? There is no soundness in you. Look at yourselves, and the matter is plain. But still you will not listen or take heed!' "

Now what is to be our attitude toward such speech? Some of us who are linguistically minded will begin to ask questions: Do we have here the correct summary of the correct translation of the original Hebrew text? Has that text suffered in transmission? What do the ancient translations into different languages have to say? And thus, while entering upon an important and yet never ending search into antiquity for the correct rendering, we actually may evade the central issue: Is this really God's Word, and does it speak to us?

Others among us will be especially interested in literary analysis. We shall marvel at the beauty of Isaiah's language, at his colorful metaphors and figures of speech, at his fearless vigor and incisive directness. Certainly he must have been a powerful preacher, we shall say! Thus, too, while pointing to an important fact, we evade the real issue.

Still others among us will analyze the literary forms in their historical setting. Did Isaiah really say all this? Later editors have often introduced material of unknown origin. We must segregate what Isaiah really said from what he did not say. Thus we find the "beat your swords into plowshares" passage given in fuller form in Micah. Now who copied from whom? Or were both copying an earlier source? The thought, however, fits a later period, so perhaps an editor inserted the passage in both. Yet, regardless of who wrote it or when, we still must face the issue. Some prophet wrote it. Is he correct; and, if so, what have his words to do with us?

Then, too, most of us are interested in historical background. What were the Israelites doing when Isaiah was speaking? Who were those terrible Assyrians, and just what did they do? What do the excavations tell us about the events of Isaiah's day? There is that cistern of Judean Lachish into which some fifteen hundred bodies were dumped. Does it actually date from about 700 B.C. when Sennacherib invaded Judah, and could those bodies actually be those of people slain in the siege? By asking and answering such questions we gather the historical facts and fix each sermon of Isaiah as nearly as possible into its setting. Is this procedure important? Certainly it is, for we must understand our history. And, while describing the events of that day accurately and minutely, we think we have met and answered all major problems. Yet still we have evaded the issue, for the history of Assyria, the history of Isaiah, the history of archeology, and the history of the Hebrews, important though they are, will never answer this basic and primary question: Amid the tumult, confusion, disillusionment, and decay of this present day, is there in Isaiah an actual word for us from the Lord, the Creator and the Ruler of this universe?

Many of us are inclined to view the old prophets as fierce, unhappy, unwholesome men. Frustrated in their own time, why should they frustrate us with their negativism and their picture of a wrathful God? After all, we must be careful of the Old Testament. Remember, it has been a most fertile source wherein texts to defend bigotry, hatred, and cruel oppression have been found! How can one reconcile the love and goodness of God with the atrocities and cruelties sanctioned by some Israelite laws? From this point of view it has well been said that the Old Testament is "a millstone around the neck of Christianity"! True, there are some good things in the book. There are clever texts and interesting stories, but those ancient men were often mistaken, and we had better not pay too much attention to their primitive literature. So again with easy consciences and proud reasoning we evade the issue. By pointing to the faults and foibles of the past we avoid those disturbing claims upon us which the words might have if seriously taken.

Thus saith the Lord:

"Woe unto them that are wise in their own eyes and prudent in their own sight!

"Woe unto them that draw iniquity with cords of falsehood, and sin as it were with a cart rope!

"Woe unto them that rise up early in the morning that they may follow strong drink, that tarry late into the night till wine inflame them, but they regard not the work of the Lord, neither have they considered the activity of his hands.

"Wash you and make you clean. Put away the evil of your doings from before mine eyes. Cease to do evil; learn to do well. If ye be willing and obedient, ye shall eat the good of the land; but if ye refuse and rebel ye shall be devoured with the sword—for the mouth of the Lord hath spoken it!"

Here again Isaiah has been speaking. Or has it really been God through him? Isaiah was conscious of speaking only to the people in his own day. But is God using those words for the quickening and saving of *us?*

Such questions immediately put us on the defensive, and mental reservations are made. Shall we actually be devoured by the sword for our evil deeds? Does God really send punishment? Did God really speak to Isaiah, or did Isaiah merely think that he did, as do many mentally unbalanced people today?

Certainty in such questions is not easy to attain, for doubt often keeps pace with faith. Yet many in our history have been absolutely sure about their answers. After the fifth century B.C., Jews believed that the Old Testament, especially the law in the first five books, had been given directly to man by God. They believed that when God took hold of a biblical writer the mind of that writer became inoperative and God worked through him by actually guiding his hand as a parent guides

the hand of a child. The mind of God, therefore, is wholly preserved in the Old Testament. No error, no mistake, could
have been introduced into the Scripture. It is God's law for
me on earth. My problem is: How am I to apply it to the
manifold activity of daily life? For live by the law I must. It
is my salvation, the "lamp unto my feet and the light unto
my path. . . . . Teach me, O Lord, the way of thy statutes, and
I shall keep it unto the end. . . . . Let my soul live and it shall
praise thee, and let thine ordinances help me!"

The Jewish people of old did not evade the issue. This is
God's Word, they tell us; man, therefore, must look to himself. But what peculiar things they often found in Scripture!
If God actually wrote this, then everything about it is important. They believed that it was even full of hidden meanings;
and to find them they used various devices, especially the
study of numbers. In Genesis, chapter 14, Abram's retainers
were 318 in number. Yet the letters in the name of Abram's
servant, Eliezer, have the value of 318, when each letter is
given its numerical value. Therefore, Abram's army must
have been made up of one man! The first word of the
Scripture begins with the second letter of the alphabet, and
not with the first. Why? There is a mystery here, a hidden
reference to the two worlds, the earthly and the heavenly, or
else a reference to the two types of law, the written and the
oral! If a letter in the sacred text was larger than the others,
or was repeated, or omitted, or had some other peculiarity due
to the inadvertence of some scribe, the rabbis were sure that it
had mystic significance. In Isa. 9:7 the Hebrew word translated "increase" begins with m. In Hebrew this letter is written one way at the end of a word, and another way elsewhere.
A scribe had accidentally written the final m at the beginning
of the word for "increase" instead of the other form of the let-

ter. Here, said a rabbi, is a mystery. Perhaps it indicates that God meant to make Hezekiah into the *M*essiah. At any rate, there is some mystic meaning hidden in that peculiar letter!

We are not convinced by this type of exegesis; but why should we not be, if Scripture is actually the Word of God? Start with that ancient theory of verbal inspiration, and we must come out in approximately the same place. The Church Fathers started with that theory and were immediately forced into difficulties. Said Origen: How do you account for all those things in Scripture which are unworthy of the Divine author? How could Moses see God's hinderparts on Mt. Sinai? That's the rankest bit of anthropomorphism—an old wife's fable! Of what value is it, he continues, for a Christian to read about the drunkenness of Noah, about Jacob and his wives and concubines, about the horrid incest of Lot, or about the foul story of Judah and Tamar? It is absurd to believe that the food laws of Leviticus are the actual Word of God for this day. Another early Christian is reported to have asked why, if the Patriarchs could have more than one wife, he could not. And so he did!

What is the answer to these things? Just this, said Origen; Scripture is a mine of wonderful and marvelous mysteries which the initiated alone can discover and unravel. The words do not really mean what they say; hence they are to be taken allegorically. Look for the hidden meanings. Of what use is it, he asks, for one who comes to the Scripture to hear what the Holy Spirit teaches the human race, to read that Abraham stood under the oak of Mamre? Mamre means "vision"; read the passage in this way, and it has a wonderful meaning. What use is it for one to be told that "the Lord opened the eyes of Agar [Hagar]"? Are we told anywhere that she closed her eyes? It is perfectly clear that the real meaning

refers to the blindness of the Jewish synagogue! Other Fathers
of the church use the same method of exegesis. That story
about the drunkenness of Noah is no mere indecent tale. It
is a figure of the death and passion of Christ (so Augustine).
The speaker in the Twenty-third Psalm is really the Church;
the shepherd is Jesus, the refreshing water is baptism. The
Song of Songs is no mere collection of poems about secular
love; it really refers to Jesus Christ and the Church!

Thus many Christians have reasoned from that day to this.
The Roman Catholics say to the Protestant: "Your trouble is
that you have no authority. You say your authority is Scripture, but Scripture can be made to mean anything." As a
prominent Catholic put it in a radio address recently: "The
Scripture says that Judas went out and hanged himself, and
another passage adds: 'Go thou and do likewise!' Put verses
together, and you can get any meaning from the Bible. You
people need someone to tell you what the Bible says, and the
Roman church does this for you." But, we may ask, how can
we be sure that the church tells us the truth? The answer must
be: Because the Scripture tells us that it does and that the
church knows and possesses *all* truth. How do you know that
the Scripture says so? Because the church says that it does!
But such reasoning around a circle is scarcely a valid or con-
vincing way to argue, especially in view of the fact that the
Catholic church and all religious organizations have been
guilty far too often of dogmatically claiming that the Bible
says what we now know it does not say.

Since the days of Martin Luther and John Calvin, Protestants have rejected the authority of the Catholic church because its errors in interpreting the Bible have indicated that it
does not know or possess all truth. With that rejection went
also the repudiation of allegory. Said Luther: "Allegories are

empty speculations, and as it were the scum of Holy Scripture"; "allegory is a sort of beautiful harlot, who proves herself specially seductive to idle men"; allegory "may degenerate into a mere monkey-game!"

And yet Protestants have been faced with the same problem with which Origen was faced. If the Scripture is actually God's word, then the whole Bible must be on one level, each part as authoritative and infallible as another (the "begats" as the "thou shalts"). So, during the centuries after the Reformers, Protestant scholars taught that inconsistencies and obscure passages must have been written by God in order to give the reader reverence and more zeal for study and to keep the profane from knowing the truth. What we do not understand, we are told, we must accept on faith. Many hold a similar position even today.

The problem of Scripture as the Word of God is indeed very real and very pressing. Now there is something within, which tells us that Isaiah is absolutely right in the basic assertions of his proclamations. We cannot entirely evade the issue. If ever God spoke to man, it is here and in similar passages throughout the Bible. There is something eternally true about this teaching, the acceptance of which is a matter of life and death, a blessing and a curse. The turmoil and tragedy of this day are adequate indications of the curse and the death which have come from our refusal to hear and to obey. But where is the line to be drawn between what is true and what is untrue, between what is God's Word and what is man's word? Who are we, mortal and erring individuals, to decide such an issue? To find suggestions for a rational decision, let us turn to Jesus and the Reformers.

The Scripture of Jesus was the Old Testament. He revered it, studied it, and frequently quoted from it. Yet the way he used it is worthy of note. He could present the Golden Rule and say: "*This* is the law and the prophets" (Matt. 7:12). The first and greatest commandments, said he, are: "Thou shalt love the Lord thy God . . . . and thou shalt love thy neighbor as thyself. On these two commandments hang all the law and the prophets" (Matt. 22:40). Here he was quoting two laws from Deut. 6:5 and Lev. 19:18 and saying that they were more important than all the rest. Now what was there in Jesus which gave him the right and the ability to say that these verses in Scripture are more important than all others; that these are a correct summary of the law, instead of, for instance, the Ten Commandments.

Jesus could say to the people: "Your Ten Commandments and your laws are not enough. Ye have heard that it was said by them of old, 'Thou shalt not kill.' . . . . But I say unto you . . . . ! Ye have heard that it was said by them of old, 'Thou shalt not commit adultery.' . . . . But I say unto you. . . . Ye have heard that it hath been said, 'An eye for an eye and a tooth for a tooth.' . . . . But I say unto you . . . . " (Matt., chap. 5). While some scholars believe that these verses were schematized or elaborated by the early church, no one can doubt Jesus' general attitude. The case is even clearer when we note how liberal he was in his view of the Sabbath (Mark 2:27) and how his view on divorce was quite different from that of the Old Testament: "It hath been said, 'Whosoever shall put away his wife, let him give her a writing of divorcement' (cf. Deut. 24:1). But I say unto you . . . ." (Matt. 5:31 f.). Again we ask: What was there in Jesus which could criticize the Scripture? It was authoritative to him and it was God's Word, but at the same time he was able to pick and to choose and to add. There was in him an inner certainty about eternal truth which enabled him to use the written law as his authority and, at the same time, to be its critic.

Turning to Martin Luther, we find the very same situation. Reading of his moral agonies, of his desperate search for peace and harmony of soul, we find that he was seeking pardon of sin, peace of conscience, and justification before God. Turning to the Bible, he found that for which he had been looking; the Scripture at once became the source of new life and new light. He went to the Bible for help and found it a never ending source of living water. And yet, peculiarly enough, he was able constantly to criticize the very source of his inspiration. He would read his Bible, come to a verse which he did not like and write opposite it: "That is not true!" And he especially disliked the Epistle of James, which to him was an "epistle of straw."

How could Luther do this? What right had he to say: "This is right and true and God's Word in Scripture, but this is not"? The old Jewish view, adopted by the Christians, gave an external authority. Everything was there, outside of a man, in black and white. To Jesus and the Reformers, apparently, the matter was not quite so simple. They approached the Bible by way of inward experience, seeking help which they desired so keenly; and they found there that which they believed with all the power of their souls to be God's Word for them and for all mankind. Evidently a Christian consciousness was at work, separating what Luther called the "wood, hay and stubble" of the Scripture from "the gold, silver, and diamonds." There was some inner apprehension of truth which brought life into an old dogma and at the same time brought the certainty that God was using the words for the salvation of a sensitive reader's soul.

Said Luther: "The Romanists [Catholics] say, 'How can

we know this or that to be true and God's Word? We must learn it from the pope and the councils.' Very well, let them decree and say what they will, still say I, thou canst not rest thy confidence thereon, nor satisfy thy conscience. *Thou must thyself decide. Thy life is at stake. Therefore, must God say unto thee in thy heart, 'This is God's Word,' else it is still undecided.*"[1] In other words, conscience is between us and the Bible—a conscience which it may be a duty to enlighten, but not a duty to disobey because God speaks to us through it.

Said Calvin: "It is acting a preposterous part to endeavor to produce sound faith in the Scripture by disputations. . . . . *The Word will never gain credit in the hearts of men till it be confirmed by the internal testimony of the Spirit.*"[1]

How do we know that the Scripture is God's Word? Said Luther: God must tell it to thee in thy heart, else it is undecided. Said Calvin: "The same Spirit who spake by the mouths of the prophets" must penetrate *our* hearts to convince us. We *know it* then to be so, just as we know how "to distinguish light from darkness, white from black, sweet from bitter."

What does all this mean? It means that those tremendous words from Isaiah are authoritative in that they inspire and save, in that they strike some kindred note within us which says, "This is true! Why do not I do something about it!" And thus throughout the Bible there speaks to us a word here and a word there which convicts us of sin, overwhelms us with the Being of the righteous and yet gracious Lord of all being, which quickens and illumines and speaks to us: "Thou *canst not* be as thou art. Arise, here is the way. Walk thou in it!"

In other words, there is an actual claim of God upon us through the Bible. Throughout the last twenty centuries this

[1] Italics are supplied by the author.

literature has been used by God for man's enlightenment. That enlightenment is not primarily concerned with science and historical facts for their own sake alone, but rather with the service and love of God. It gives no dogma about a mechanical or external authority of each section or every word or the whole Bible at once, but it rather focuses upon that one particular portion at a time which arrests us and convicts us of our sin. The real authority of the Bible lies in those moral and spiritual truths which reach the believer's heart. It is not those historical and scientific truths for which we have been given logical faculties, minds, to discern and prove.[2]

There is a freedom in this point of view, therefore, to find *the Word behind the words*. Does Isaiah speak to us directly from God? Well, we say, he was a man who lived in his time and spoke to his time, and his day is not our day. True, but what were the great, searching, basic propositions of Isaiah's proclamations? What is the Word behind the words? The first chapter of Genesis represents the science of that day, we say. It cannot be our science, and it cannot be squared with all that we now know about the way God made the world. True, but let us not evade the issue! The basic assertions there are of God the Creator and of man in God's image. What about those assertions? Are they true or untrue? Decide this day and act accordingly! Thus speaks the biblical writer to us. The book of Jonah tells us about a man who was swallowed by a great fish and lived in its belly for three days and three nights. Could that have happened or could it not have happened? Whales are big enough, but could a man live after such an experience, we ask? But there we are, again in danger of evading the

[2] For an elaboration of this view see Arthur A. Hays, "The Ultimate Basis for the Authority of Scripture According to Calvin," in L. G. Leary (ed.), *From the Pyramids to Paul* (New York: Thomas Nelson & Sons, 1935), pp. 79 ff.

issue! Here is a fretful, querulous prophet, half-heartedly and whiningly bearing a word from God to his own and his people's worst enemy. God says to him: "You have had concern for a gourd-vine which might have saved you a headache. Why should not I have concern for Nineveh wherein are 120,000 people who cannot tell right from wrong?" Behind the mere words and framework of that story is there not an eternal Word given to us by the Determiner of Destiny out of sheer love and grace? In this ancient literature has there been a breaking of the eternal into the temporal? To be sure, the temporal is there, and we must find and discuss it. Yet such discussions may become a means of sin among us, whereby we avoid the searching, disturbing, searing truth of the eternal.

To be sure, there are many valid and important, yet nevertheless external and secondary, arguments for the uniqueness of biblical literature. Calvin pointed to "the heavenliness of the matter, the efficacy of the doctrine. . . . , the scope of the whole, the full discovery it makes of the only way of man's salvation." It is true, of course, that other religions have had inspired insights; but the completeness of this biblical revelation reveals how partial and piecemeal is the revelation elsewhere. All of this becomes the more remarkable in the light of modern archeological discovery. Here in the covers of this one Book we know now that we actually have the cream of the literature which the ancient East produced. Thousands of documents of every sort have been unearthed which can be compared with biblical literature and which help us greatly in understanding it. Yet amid the glorious ruins of Egypt, Syria, and Mesopotamia one still must stand amazed at the literary, poetic, and religious genius of Israel. The other nations had nothing which can be placed on the same level with the Bible. Israel lived in that ancient world, borrowed widely from it, and yet trans-

formed all that was borrowed. Her literature, while produced
in that world, was never quite of it.

Such arguments as these are attractive. They magnify the
importance of the book; and volume upon volume can be, and
is being, produced about the Bible as literature and, further,
about the English Bible as the classic of English prose style.
But at such a point of praise we are often inclined to stop. Are not
these verses from Isaiah more than fine, beautiful, inspired literature? If there is within them a veritable Word from God,
shall we listen or not? This is not a literature to be taken lightly. We cannot read it as mere litterateurs, technicians, or historians and really expect to understand it. Biblical literature is
what it is because it was written by men who were standing in a
fevered, restless, chaotic world, men who were seeking the answer to the meaning of existence and struggling to find their
place in the sum of things. Actually, to find the eternal truth
amid the temporal requires that we be no mere grandstand ob-
servers. We, too, are sinning and suffering and sorrowing and
standing beneath the judgment, and withal the grace, of the
Almighty. The Word behind the words is to be found only by
those who are conscious of their position—nay, predicament—
in life and who examine the facts of that life as did the prophets. After all, Scripture is of little value, except for antiquarian
purposes, unless it affords the reader a quickening of spirit, a
searching of heart, and a cleansing of soul. The searching,
sensitive, thoughtful reader must ever be brought to the point
of praying as did Jeremiah:

Though our iniquities testify against us, O Lord, work thou for thy
name's sake; for many are our backslidings; against thee have we sinned.
The hope of Israel [art thou] O Lord, its Savior in time of trouble. Why
shouldst thou be as a stranger in the land, as a traveler who turneth aside to
lodge for a night . . . . ? Thou, O Lord, art in the midst of us. By thy name
we are called—leave us not! [Jer. 14:7–9].

Such must be the attitude of every man who humbly seeks for the Word behind the words. With this in mind let us examine again our Old Testament and inquire into the meaning of its basic assertions.

Before doing so, however, we should point out that there are many who heartily agree with the point of view here expressed and who say: This is just the point. Let us get at the eternal and abiding, and leave the history aside. Why should we concern ourselves with the history at all?

But if we adopt such an attitude, we miss the very genius of the Old Testament. There is a Word behind the words, but it is one which is made concrete and vivid in historical events. We find here no mere theorizing of the spectator but the observation of actual history in order that a warning and a lesson from God may be found for the guidance of the writer and his people. Here God's revelation is made relevant and real by concrete situations. The prophets know nothing of an abstract principle of truth. They know only of God's revelation in the natural and human world. Disregard the history, and we should have left in prophetic religion little but meaningless abstractions which we ourselves have made. We shall examine this history, therefore, with special reference to the prophetic view of its significance.

CHAPTER II

"CHOOSE YOU THIS DAY": THE MEANING OF HISTORY

THE word "crisis" is very popular in recent theology; in fact, it has been used so much that some have become rather weary of it. Yet it is a good word, possessing at this moment of world history an especial significance. Today in this planetary crisis, we are witnessing the bankruptcy and failure of our meager attempts at erecting a better world. After the first World War our eyes were turned upon utopia, symbolized in the League of Nations, but our actions were so filled with selfishness, and consequently so waterlogged with inertia, that it is small wonder that we were again forced into war.

This situation accentuates the continual crisis in personal life, one which leaves most men of good will restless and disturbed. Among Christians there is an uneasiness with regard to the gospel and with regard to the manner in which it is to be presented to the world. We struggle to teach, preach, and live—above all, live—the good life, as "saints amidst Caesar's household." Many church members derive great comfort from this effort, as indeed we all do, forgetting that good works alone can save no man. Here we stand in the midst of social unrest, in the midst of the Negro problem, in the midst of exploitation, governmental dishonesty and incompetence, alcoholism, militarism, prostitution, and all the rest. Yet this is a Christian nation, and our churches continue their preaching about the "religious life," extolling this nation under God

17

and exhorting us to love our fellows. Somehow our Christian activity has not bitten deep into the evil of this country in a manner commensurate with our numbers. There has been a timidity, a tendency toward irrelevant and superficial preaching, and even a tendency toward Phariseeism in our presentation of the gospel. And we now see our failure.

I suppose that many a minister during the last two decades has drawn heavily upon the same gamut of preaching themes as has this one. There was the social gospel—an exceedingly important emphasis—but it failed to get at the personal roots of social life and soon appeared shallow and one-sided. There was also character education, and the emphasis upon "the deeper resources within." There was the attempt to reconcile science and religion, including the emphasis upon the correct ways of thinking about God (he is no longer a bearded grandfather!). Yet these emphases and many others, while valid, appear trivial in the midst of what we are now facing. How can we at this time present the searching claims of the gospel so that men will listen, take heed, and be changed thereby? Our ecclesiasticism is not enough. Filling churches is not enough. Our human righteousness is not enough—not when it is brought face to face with the righteousness of God, as it is in this day.

All the foregoing merely adds to the uneasiness about life itself, for the business of living is often but a sickness unto death. The struggle to attain, to "win friends and influence people," and to satisfy the various desires of the ego leaves one frustrated and restless. What are we trying to accomplish? After all, we are soon to die. To be sure, the specter of death is usually pushed into the background, and we live as though the present were eternal. But death remains the one major event to which few of us can adjust ourselves successfully. It remains on the border line of consciousness, rising to plague us when we are too weak to crowd it out. Yet there it is, and it must some day be faced. Certainly, we walk daily on a narrow ridge between time and eternity and may at any moment stumble into the unknown. Yet most of us, refusing to face this particular reality, attempt to live as though this world, which in a sense is only our tent, were really our home. And so we continually seek, but never quite find; we struggle and strive for those things which we want, but we are never really satisfied. Life is one continual series of crises. We cry for peace, when there is no peace—peace of conscience, of spirit, of society! We long for happiness, security, and contentment, but where on this earth or in this life are they to be found? Like the Israelites in Sinai we are constantly murmuring, rebellious, and uneasy.

Thus in a world of crisis and a life full of turmoil we turn to the Old Testament. What do we find? Do we find good *ideas*, platitudes, abstract theological theorizing? Do we find many examples of that type of religious homily, so filled (to quote Shakespeare) "with such a deal of skimble-skamble stuff as puts men from their faith"? The answer is "No"—not when the writing is properly understood. There are three main themes running through the Old Testament or, for that matter, throughout the whole Bible: *God, human sin, and redemption*. For this reason the Cross has stood through the centuries and still stands today as the one symbol which adequately summarizes biblical religion. On the one hand, it illustrates the nature of human sin, sin which can crucify the Savior of this world. On the other, it represents the purpose and the power of God to redeem man from that sin—not necessarily to deliver him from the consequences of it but to lift him above the tragedy of it.

In the Old Testament we find these themes appearing and reappearing in all but a few of the shorter or "marginal" books; and they are always presented concretely, not abstractly. They appear in great sermons, many of which when studied carefully in their setting can still fill the reader with fear and trembling. The prophets do not write as theologians. They give us the great certainties of faith as seen in relation to the crises of their time. We find these great themes also in the prayers of troubled people, in hymns of praise, and especially in stories of individuals and of the Hebrew people.

Now what do we discover to be the purport of all this writing? Is it to recount great exploits or please the ear with pleasant words? Taking the Old Testament as a whole, we find that it is rather to get people to recognize and obey the revealed will of their Lord. Do the Israelite writers produce their sermons, psalms, and stories in the easy and quiet manner of men enjoying peace and prosperity and security? Quite the contrary. Throughout the Old Testament we meet one crisis after another and continuous turmoil, tragedy, and frustration. To be sure, there is the beautiful, quiet Twenty-third Psalm, but the peace of that poem and of others like it was achieved only through a tremendous venture of faith in the living, righteous God, while the writer walked in the presence of his enemies "through the valley of the shadow of death." Indeed, when one stops to think about it, the theology of Israel was born in and of continual crisis; it was created by, and in turn created, crisis. The Hebrew people, like all people everywhere, wanted rest, happiness, and peace. They were engaged, just as are we, in a desperate search for security, shelter, and safety among the destructive forces, both economic and political, of their world. Instead of finding that which they sought, they were continually faced with turmoil, social upheaval, war, and defeat.

Let us examine the history from this point of view. In the very first verses of Genesis we find a key for the unlocking of the whole story. "In the beginning God created the heavens and the earth" out of the watery waste of the "deep." In other words, he was creating order out of disorder, cosmos out of chaos. And throughout the Bible we have the story of God's action in history, of his struggle with the recalcitrant will of man to bring order into the latter's chaotic soul and society. Little wonder, then, that the Old Testament presents us with a continuous series of crises!

In the Garden of Paradise man wilfully disobeyed and found that the penalty was separation from God and from Paradise; and that in turn meant toil, suffering, and hardship. In the story of the Flood we learn of the disastrous consequences of man's wickedness. God is righteous, and to man in every age that righteousness is "a consuming fire." Yet suffering was not the end, for after the Flood came the rainbow, to the religious eye of a good Israelite an everlasting symbol of Divine grace.

There in those stories we are taught the central elements of an Israelite's faith: God and his righteousness, man's suffering and toil brought upon him by disobedience, and withal the ever present rainbow—God's gracious revelation of himself for the salvation of men. Did Adam and Eve really live? Was there really a Garden and a Flood? It is important for us to have an answer to these questions. Yet we must also read these stories as they were meant by their authors to be read. Presumably, everyone in that day believed that the stories were more or less literally true. The only reason the writers had for retelling them was to teach religion through the crises of man's history. And what profound insight into the nature of life they contain! That judgment passed upon man at the conclusion of the story of the Flood ("For that the imagination of man's heart is evil from his youth . . . ." [Gen. 8:21]) remains a statement of truth which a sentimental age will continually minimize.

So the story moves on to the patriarchs, the sojourn, and the conquest. Most dramatic is the oppression and slavery in Egypt. Here the Hebrew people who settled in Goshen were faced with the greatest trial of their existence; but it was to those terrible days that the Israelite nation later traced its origin. The basic tenets of Israel's religion and the covenant bond between the people and their God, which for centuries was the main tie holding the several Hebrew tribes together, came into being in that time of insecurity, fear, and anxiety.

Many of the Hebrews who left Egypt were sure they would soon enter into a land of milk and honey. Instead they encountered trouble, hardship, and more trouble. Faced with a scarcity of water, they wished they had remained in Egypt where at least there was plenty to drink. Then they were provided with water, but soon found that they were hungry. So they were given manna to eat (a honey-like substance which still drops from tamarisk trees in Sinai). Yet soon they were tired of manna, and again they murmured and wept: "Who shall give us flesh to eat? We remember the fish which we did eat in Egypt free of charge, the melons, and the leeks, and the onions, and the garlic. But now our soul is dried away. There is nothing at all save this manna to look upon!" (Num. 11:4–5.) So they were given quail to eat, and the people fell upon the quail, and many apparently became sick with acute indigestion or something of the sort! Some of them became rebellious and said to Moses and Aaron: "Ye take too much upon you. All of this community is holy. . . . . Why then do you lift yourselves up above the Lord's assembly!" Others said: "Let us make us a captain and return to Egypt!" In their midst stood Moses and the few who were loyal to him, accomplishing tremendous feats of spiritual strength and, in spite of continued anxiety and rebellion, gradually leading the troubled flock to the Promised Land.

It would be difficult to find a more dramatic account of a people in crisis. Indeed, it would be difficult to find a more vivid illustration of the tragic dilemma of life itself. People are like that! Murmuring, grumbling, groaning, refusing to follow provided leadership, always wanting to do something different from what they are doing, to be where they are not (the pastures are always greener on the other side of the fence), seeking, seeking, but never quite finding—such were the Hebrews in Sinai, and just so are we. We are always at odds with ourselves and our surroundings, a "people bent on backsliding."

Yet the crises in the wilderness were merely a beginning of what was to come. The Promised Land was no haven of security. During the days of the Judges "there was no king in Israel; every man did that which was right in his own eyes." This political and moral chaos was made worse by the constant inroads of "oppressors," the most dangerous of whom proved to be the Philistines, who by 1050 B.C. were able to place most of Israel in almost complete subjection. So the scattered groups united, and for a brief period enjoyed a golden age under the leadership of the energetic and colorful David and Solomon. Yet even during those eighty years the country was rocked by disaffection and rebellion, with the result that it split into two groups upon Solomon's death.

Then came the bickering between the groups, political disorder in the north which at times verged on anarchy, social chaos and upheaval, religious revolutions, and finally the Assyrian and Babylonian invasions which brought the political existence of the two kingdoms to an end and meant the exile of the intellectual and well-to-do classes. The result was poverty and disorder in Palestine, while many of the exiled sat by the rivers of Syria and Babylon and wept when they remembered Zion.

Never in world history has there been a half-millennium more filled with turmoil, tragedy, and continued disturbance of the established order. And this was the day in which the great prophets lived.

Now these prophets were certainly uninterested in merely good ideas, platitudes, or theological theorizing. They were no "armchair" or "grandstand" philosophers of history. On the contrary, they were men who were absorbed in the issues of their time, analyzing them with acute awareness of a divine mission. Their intellectual and spiritual faculties were finely sharpened and keenly focused upon God, his ways in the past, and his demands for the present. In sharp contrast to the earlier "sons of the prophets," their inspiration did not leave them babbling and incoherent with depression of mental faculties. Instead, their intellectual powers were tremendously heightened, and they spoke more, not less, intelligibly. Their observations of men and movements of the day were keen and astute. But their concern was not with mere analysis and observation. It was rather to seek conviction and repentance by proclamation of the Word of the Lord for that specific, historical moment. The resulting combination of all factors made their sermons fiery, brilliant, beautiful, and exceedingly powerful.

Nevertheless, the very fact that this prophetic proclamation is directed to specific conditions and events makes it the more difficult to use. One can read the words and discover fine phrases and incisive ideas and thus be able to generalize on the teaching of the prophets. In so doing, however, he will miss the power of a preaching that was meant to *convert*. Only careful study of the historical situation to which the prophet was directing himself can reveal his true purpose. Trained as he was to discover the movement of God behind the political, social, and religious events of the past, he proclaimed to the people that the events of that moment meant thus and so. Therefore, repent and change your ways, ye people. The Day of the Lord is at hand!

Isaiah and Jeremiah may be taken as familiar examples. At the very beginning and throughout their ministries a primary element was a sense of crisis and impending doom. With it was a desperate anxiety for the fate of their people and a vivid consciousness of the central role which they, as God's spokesmen, were to play in that crisis.

A large section of Isaiah's prophecies cluster around the period of the Assyrian siege of Judah in 701–700 B.C. The prophet's concern was to explain the meaning of those events, the reasons for them, and their ultimate issue. What do these things mean? The Assyrian is the chastening rod of the Lord's anger, even though he does not know it but says: "By the strength of my hand have I done it, and by my wisdom" (chap. 10). To be sure, this sinful agent will soon have to pay for his own deeds, but in the meantime he is used by God for the punishing of the Chosen People. And why should the Lord deal thus with Judah? "Hear, O heavens, and give ear, O earth; for the Lord hath spoken: 'I have nourished and brought up children and they have rebelled against me. . . . . The ox knoweth his owner, and the ass his master's crib; [but]

Israel doth not know, my people doth not consider.' Ah, sinful nation, a people laden with iniquity. . . . . They have forsaken the Lord and have provoked the Holy One of Israel unto anger. . . . .Why should ye be stricken any more? Ye will revolt more and more. The whole head is sick. . . . . From the sole of the foot even unto the head there is no soundness in you. . . . . Your country is desolate; your cities are burned with fire; your land—strangers devour it" (chap. 1).

What can you do about it? "Turn ye unto him, O children of Israel, against whom ye have deeply revolted. . . . . Then shall the Assyrian fall by the sword, not of man—and a sword, not of man, shall devour him" (31:6–8). "If ye be willing and obedient, ye shall eat the good of the land, but if ye refuse and rebel, ye shall be devoured with the sword, for the mouth of the Lord hath spoken it!" (1:19–20.)

The political implication of these views is, of course, that Judah must submit and pay tribute. That, indeed, is what she ultimately had to do. Yet in the back of Isaiah's mind is that basic prophetic doctrine that the people of Israel and Judah were not called by God to develop powerful, "cultured" nations after the pattern of Solomon, flitting around in the political world "like a silly dove" or acting like "a cake not turned." Rather, they were called upon to establish a sound social and economic life under God. They were a unique and special people, and "worldly" wisdom, wealth, and power were not God's will or gift to them. And in the description of the precise way in which they are violating their true mission at every historical crossroad, Isaiah and all the prophets are most vivid and specific.

Similarly, Jeremiah in the whirl of the events surrounding the final destruction of the Judean state proclaimed with desperate urgency that the hand of God was behind the crisis and that the occasion called for national repentance. "Thus saith the Lord of hosts, the God of Israel: 'Behold, I shall bring upon this city and upon all her towns the full calamity that I pronounced against it because they have stiffened their necks in order that they might not hear my words'" (19:15). Why? "An appalling and horrible thing has come to pass in the land. The prophets prophesy falsely and the priests rule at their [the prophets'] direction. And my people love to have it so. But what will ye do in the end thereof?" (5:30–31.) " 'Woe unto the shepherds that destroy and scatter the sheep of my pasture!' saith the Lord" (23:1). "Woe unto him [King Jehoiakim] that buildeth his house by unrighteousness, and his chambers by wrong. . . . . Thine eyes and thine heart are not but for thy covetousness, and for to shed innocent blood, and for oppression, and for violence, to do it. . . . . Thus saith the Lord: 'Execute ye justice and righteousness. Deliver the spoiled out of the hand of the oppression and do no wrong; do no violence to the stranger, the fatherless, nor the widow. . . . . But if ye will not hear these words, I swear by myself,' saith the Lord, 'that this house shall become a desolation. . . . .' And many nations shall pass by this city, and they shall say every man to his neighbor, 'Wherefore hath the Lord done thus unto this great city?' Then people will say: 'Because they have forsaken the covenant of the Lord their God, and worshipped other gods and served them' " (22:13 ff., 3 ff.). "Thus saith the Lord: "Behold, I have set before you the way of life and the way of death. He that abideth in this city shall die by the sword and by the famine and by the pestilence; but he that goeth out and falleth [surrendereth] to the Chaldeans that besiege you, he shall live. . . . . For I have set my face against this city for evil ["distress "or "calamity," not ethical evil] and

not for good. . . . . It shall be given into the hand of the king
of Babylon and he shall burn it with fire" (21:8–10).

This is by no means all that these prophets had to say, but it
illustrates their method of approach to the crises of their time.
They were not preachers concerned only with individual piety
or the "spiritual glow." Nor were they metaphysicians or
philosophers of history or astute political economists. Rather
they were radical, religious revolutionaries, steeped in the
knowledge of the God of their fathers, focusing the great sum
of that knowledge upon the political and economic crisis of the
age. History is no mere story of human activity to be viewed,
dissected, and described as one would analyze mathematical
statistics. It is the arena of the creative activity of the living,
righteous, holy God—a God whose works permit no description apart from a clarion call to repentance and conversion,
even on the part of the one who is dissecting them.

At this point we may do well to pause in order to ask why it
is that so much of the current writing and teaching about
Israel's prophets appears so stereotyped, platitudinous, and
dull. There has been a veritable stream of books about them,
and after reading a few one can almost guess what the next is
going to say, except for the variations in treatment of the
critical problems involved. The answer would appear to lie in
the assumption that the important thing about any religion
lies almost solely in the area of belief, that in treating the
prophets our job is to abstract their beliefs, analyze them, and
trace the genetic history of each in order to determine its
growth and validity. Any unique features possessed by the
prophets are largely assumed to lie in the wonderful ideas
which they held.[1]

[1] On this point see further the excellent and important article of Paul S.
Minear, "The Conception of History in the Prophets and Jesus," *Journal of Bible
and Religion*, XI, No. 3 (1943), 156 ff.

This is a valid, necessary, and laudable endeavor which has resulted in the liberation of the prophets from the dogmatic, and typological treatment which once obscured not only their real message but their commanding importance as well. Yet such a point of view is limited and, indeed, false when it claims that it thus actually understands these men. Isaiah and Jeremiah were not conscious of, or even especially interested in, presenting novel ideas or beliefs or in testing the validity of what they held true by objective analysis or dissection. Their main interest was in the immediate word from God, intended for the people's instant acceptance. It was a word which was meant to confront the people with the will of God for that particular moment of crisis. Make abstractions of the ideas, and we divorce them from the reality which brought them forth and gave them relevance. Separate the idea of God in the Bible from the direct, immediate encounter with him, and we are lost in irrelevant, expansive vacuity.

There are two conditions which must be met before we can really understand the prophets in the sense that they meant their own messages to be understood. The first is that we be willing to stand with them at their point of vantage, look at their particular history with them, and experience the challenge and immediacy of the will of God for that moment. The second is that we endeavor to stand in our own history, struggle with the same tragic and compelling events which concern us, and strive with sensitive souls and inspired intelligence to find the immediate Word of the Lord for *us*, now, at this moment. The justice and righteousness of which the prophets spoke will always remain general, abstract, and unexciting unless we are willing to meet these two conditions while reading about them.

A contemporary writer has perceived the true nature of

Israel's history and therewith its significance for this age and every age:

> In the Bible . . . . we find men in one crisis after another, seeking earnestly to know the will of God and to do accordingly; men who were fighting for their very existence, ready to listen to the judgments and promises of the Determiner of destiny. They were not spectators of an interesting drama for the sake of amusement or out of mere intellectual curiosity. They were anxious and often desperate participants in a vital struggle, concerned with their food, shelter and safety, against the destructive forces among and around them. Recent theology has opened our eyes to the seriousness of our own situation. It has constrained us to recognize that we also are involved in a life and death struggle. It has forced us to fix our minds upon the economic distresses of our time, upon exploitation and oppression in our midst, upon the sins and sufferings involved in the "labor problem" or the "race problem," upon the tyranny and enslavement which have turned our world into a valley of the shadow of death. We also are living in a day of judgment. We also are anxious to know the signs of the times. We also are looking anxiously into the past and into our future. We also must choose between good and evil, between life and death.

> Thus we have discovered a new kinship between us and the Biblical people. We can once again recognize them as men like us, or ourselves as a bewildered and anxious people like them. We find that they sinned and sorrowed as we do; that they sought after their God, and prayed and repented before Him as we ought to do; that they received the judgments and threats and promises of God with "fear and awful reverence" as we ought to do. We now care much more for what God said to Amos in the midst of luxury and oppression, or to Hosea in the midst of killing, stealing, and trust in kings and princes, or to Jeremiah in a besieged city, than we do for the evolution of Hebrew ideas from Amos to Jeremiah. Let him who sits in his ease and complacency study the gradual improvement of Hebrew ideals. But one who stands surrounded by oppression and tyranny, by tumult and confusion, by fire and the sword; one who cares for the people and their cry of pain and fear; one who is trembling for his own soul and life, let such a man inquire if there be a Word from Jehovah.[2]

It is thus evident that in the Old Testament there is little history for history's sake, but a religious interpretation of history in which there is a continuing encounter between men and

[2] Joseph Haroutunian, "Recent Theology and the Biblical Mind," *Journal of Bible and Religion*, VIII, No. 1 (February, 1940), 20.

God, an encounter which compels decision. The turmoil and suffering of the nation confronted the writers with such problems as these: Why do these things happen to us? Why does God allow them to happen? Are we not his people? Did he not choose us out from the nations of the world, deliver us from bondage, and give us this good land of Canaan to use and to enjoy? Then why does he make us to suffer and to eat our bread in bitterness? It was with these questions in mind that they combed their past. They approached their task with a basic assumption. History is important because God *is;* he is its Ruler, the Determiner of its final issue, the One who gives it significance. He is to be found behind all the events of life, controlling them, revealing his will through them, and determined that he shall reign supreme in the hearts of men.

The books of Judges and Kings are clear illustrations of the results obtained when this point of view was applied to the crises of Israel's past. They gave conclusive proof of that basic biblical proposition: disloyalty to the Lord brings national ruin, while loyalty to him is the only means of national salvation. If Israel had only remained true to the Lord its God! Instead, as the Preface to the Book of Judges (2:11—3:6) carefully explains, the people "forsook the Lord, the God of their Fathers, who brought them out of the land of Egypt, and they followed other gods, of the gods of the people that were round about them, and provoked the Lord to anger!" The framework of the Book of Judges is a series of cycles of infidelity, punishment through a foreign oppressor, repentance, the raising-up of a judge as deliverer, and finally rest, during which there is again infidelity.

The Books of Kings were edited from a similar viewpoint. Every king is tested by the norm of his exclusive loyalty to God and to the central sanctuary in Jerusalem. Why was it that the kingdom split apart after Solomon's death? The editor finds the clue in the fact that Solomon had so many wives, for whose foreign gods he was willing to erect altars (I Kings 11:4–6). Small wonder that Israel fell to the Assyrians in 721 B.C., for every king in the Northern Kingdom was found to have done "that which was evil in the sight of the Lord"! Few even of the Judean kings escape censure, though here there were exceptions, among whom the most notable was Josiah (seventh century): "And like unto him was there no king before him who turned to the Lord with all his heart and with all his soul and with all his might . . . ." (II Kings 23:25).

The effect is a solemn and impressive presentation of the working of the righteous God in history. This is the conviction which is the connecting thread of the Old Testament, and as a result Israel's history is "holy history." No other people of the ancient Near East were so keenly aware of the crises of their past as instances of Divine judgment and punishment. This is the main factor which raises this literature high above that of the surrounding nations and places it in a category by itself. Watch the crises of our past, say the authors, for it is in them that the revelation of God's will is to be seen in all its power and majesty.

Of course, it is easy to criticize this type of historical writing. Modern historians would call it propaganda, and that is exactly what it is—religious propaganda written for the edification and correction of the people. But does this fact destroy its validity? In one sense it can be, and often has been, held, by such men as Voltaire, that this writing of history is execrable. Here is the beginning of the distortion of history for dogmatic ends—a condition of affairs which existed, for the most part, until the Enlightenment of the seventeenth and eighteenth centuries. Dogma, religion, and history became so mixed with one another as to cause such a man as Benjamin Jowett of the last century to write that he was "determined not to submit to this abominable system of terrorism, which prevents the statement of the plainest facts, and makes true theology or theological education impossible." Theological bias can obscure and misinterpret facts, and this certainly happened in Judges and Kings. The judges, we now know, did not judge one after another, as represented by the editor of the book; some were contemporaneous. Political and economic forces at work in the period were so subordinated as to misrepresent the actual historical significance of the men. Further, in the Books of Kings certain important rulers have very little said about them, Omri and Jeroboam II, for example, apparently because their reigns contained little material which illustrated the editor's thesis. In addition, Zimri, who reigned but seven days before he was killed by Omri, scarcely had time "to do that which was evil in the sight of the Lord" in the national and religious sense which the writer had in mind.

Such argument about details, however, is evasion of the real issue. To notice misinterpretation of some fact is one thing, but to deny the validity of the point of view is quite another. Is history the scene of the Divine judgment? Many historians and philosophers have joined forces to drive the theological moralist off the field. One of them has said: "The most useless and unproductive of all forms of reflection—the dispensing of moral judgments upon people or upon actions in retrospect" —is the type of historical writing here under consideration.

Now, of course, it is true that we cannot easily classify all men and nations as saints or sinners by any narrow moral standard. Certainly, many priests in Israel (against whom the prophets reacted) were using a very narrow basis of judgment when they believed that a people to be prosperous must sacrifice in just this manner and not that. But let a man who believes in God get away from the *basic* contention of Israel's theologians if he can! They reiterated time and again in Kings that if you want to know more about the facts, you must go to this source or to that ("The Acts of Solomon," "The Chronicles of the Kings of Israel," or "The Chronicles of the Kings of Judah"); but if you want to know what these things mean, we will tell you. It is "righteousness which exalteth a nation, but sin is a reproach to any people." "Behold," exclaims one writer, "I call heaven and earth to witness against you this day. Life and death I have placed before you, the blessing and the curse. Therefore, choose life that you may live, you and your seed, by loving the Lord thy God, by hearkening unto his voice, and by holding fast to him, for he is your life and the extension of your days!" (Deut. 30:19-20.)

Let a man start where these writers started, venturing a belief in God as the Lord of human destiny, and how can he come to any other conclusion? History must be significant! Crisis, turmoil, and suffering are themselves evidences of its significance. Let a people hearken unto the commandments of God and order their lives and society accordingly; then that people will be exalted. Let them disobey those commandments, and they are sure to be brought low. Every crisis in human history is man's God-given opportunity to repent, to turn again from his evil way that he may live.

The Chinese word for "crisis," as the writer was recently informed, is composed of two elements: *wei*, meaning "danger," and *chi*, meaning "opportunity." That is precisely the Hebrew view. Every danger, every humiliation, every period of suffering, is a time of opportunity. "History is no sad paean of woe," exlaims an English writer; "it is rather a reiterated call to repentance."

But there is even a deeper truth here. Throughout, the Bible portrays God's attempt to erect order out of disorder and the frustration of that attempt by man's continuing effort to erect a Tower of Babel and live as though he himself were Lord. How can his blindness and self-centered egotism, which in truth are destroying him, be overcome that he may learn his true role on earth? God speaks here and reveals himself there, but man on his tower will not hearken. Hence the necessity of crises! Israel's anxiety and restlessness in the Wilderness were the very road to the Promised Land. Judah's Exile meant a golden age of great literature, and in addition the moral elevation of a whole group. It does seem as though man cannot thrive in the prosperity he constantly seeks. He will humbly learn of God and resolve to be obedient only when faced with hardship, suffering, and death. God's revelation to man appears most effective in periods of the latter's weakness. The biblical gospel is one of salvation, directed to the deep disharmony and friction in the human soul and society. God the Redeemer of man the sinner is the concern of biblical religion from start to finish. Israel's history, conceived as a series of God-sent or God-used crises, may therefore be far more significant than many another history made up of "objective" facts, for here we have a key to the meaning of human life. The frustration and tragedy of life is man's opportunity, for God is the Lord of history! "Now therefore reverence the Lord and serve him in sincerity and in truth, and put away the gods which your fathers served. . . . . And if it seem evil unto you to serve the Lord, choose you this day whom ye will serve. . . . . As for me and my house, we will serve the Lord" (Josh. 24:14–15).

CHAPTER III

"OBEY MY VOICE": A CHAPTER ON TERMINOLOGY

WE ARE now to look deeper into the religious faith of Israel by examining briefly some of the basic terms which the Old Testament employs. As we noted in the last chapter, prophetic religion was vitally concerned with the crises of life and the interpretation of their meaning for the present and the future of Israelite history. The deeper rootage and fundamental tenets of the faith have been frequently misunderstood and misinterpreted because we have often failed to pierce the veil of its terminology.

Theology is almost inevitably anthropomorphic. After all, we are human, created beings, and we possess a language which is limited to our human understanding. Thus, when we speak about God and our relation to him, we are forced to use terms which are familiar and real; and these are usually derived from our social relationships. Modern Christianity, taking its cue from the New Testament, generally conceives of the relationship between God and man as between a benevolent father and his son or his children. God is a Father, and, as a father loves his children and the children the father, so God loves us and we should love him.

In the Old Testament this father-son picture is rare. The basic proposition there is that God is our Lord, our Master, our Sovereign, our Ruler. "Lord" as a synonym for God is still popular among us, and we have inherited it from the religious vocabulary of Israel. The conception of God as ruling Lord is clearly to be seen in the story of Gideon, who is said to have told the people who would make him a king: "I will not rule over you; nor shall my son rule over you. *Jehovah rules over you!*" (Judg. 8:23.) Isaiah, in that disturbing vision at the beginning of his career, "saw the Lord sitting upon a throne, high and lifted up," and he exclaimed: "Woe is me! For I am undone, because I am a man of unclean lips, and I dwell in the midst of a people of unclean lips. *For mine eyes have seen the King, Jehovah of hosts*" (Isa., chap 6). Many other passages illustrate the conception, for example, "How beautiful upon the mountains are the feet of him that bringeth good tidings, that publisheth peace, ... that saith unto Zion, *Thy God reigneth!*" (Isa. 52:7.) The Christian conception of the "Kingdom" of God is thus to be understood as arising out of this background. "Lord," "Ruler," "King," are primary contributions of Israel to the Christian terminology about God.

Of course, there are other terms which are occasionally used in the Old Testament. The Twenty-third Psalm, for example, pictures God as a "shepherd"; but kings and rulers in the ancient East, where keepers of flocks and herds were common, were often called the "shepherds" of their people, and we should expect to find that term applied to the Ruler of Israel. Jehovah is also judge, lawgiver, savior, the source of equity; but these also were the functions of a ruler. Thus: "For the Lord is our judge; the Lord is our statute-giver; the Lord is our king; he will save us" (Isa. 33:22). The prophet Hosea introduced an entirely new picture into the scene when he conceived of God as the "Husband" of the adulterous wife, Israel. Such a conception, while it was popular among certain religious leaders for a time, was apparently inadequate and soon ceased to be widely used.

Many today believe that here we have one of the basic faults of Old Testament religion. God there is a fear-inspiring Ruler, whereas in the New Testament he is a loving Father. We shall return to this belief again, but at the moment we should remember the day in which the Israelites lived. We note in a number of passages that they could and did think occasionally of God as a Father: "But now, O Lord, thou art our Father; we are the clay and thou art our potter and we are the work of thy hand" (Isa. 64:8). "A son honoreth his father and a servant his master. If then I am a Father, where is mine honor? And if I am a Master, where is my fear? saith the Lord of hosts . . . ." (Mal. 1:6). In the first passage God is conceived as a Father in the sense that he is the Creator. In the second we see the two conceptions, Father and Master, side by side, and the prophet is implying that the practical outcome of both for the believer should be a proper attitude toward God and obedience to his will. In other words, Malachi is conscious of the fact that these are merely terms and that what we call God is of small importance as compared to our attitude toward him.

By the sixth and fifth centuries Israelites were apparently familiar with the term "father" as applied to God, but before that time the religious leaders were chary about its use. And they had good reason to be! In the world around them the transition from nomadic to settled agricultural life had brought about a change in the conceptions of the tribal gods, so that they were altered to culture and nature deities. In consequence, the "fatherhood" of a god was apparently conceived as more of a *physical* than a personal and ethical relationship. From the tenth century on it became increasingly popular for parents to name a child "son" or "daughter" of this or that god or goddess. We are reminded of Jeremiah's denunciation of idolators as those who say "to the tree you are my father, and to the stone you have borne me!" (Jer. 2:27.)

No Israelite theologian could have tolerated such an idea. Jehovah to them was no physical father with wife and children like the other gods! Among the Israelite names in the Old Testament there is not a single example of one meaning "son (or daughter) of Jehovah" or of any other god. The religious leaders of Israel did not dare to use the term "father" in this connection until the great battle with polytheism had been largely won.[1] Those of us who have been making hasty criticisms of the Old Testament for its "fear-inspiring Ruler" should remember this fact in order that we may resist idolatry in our day as they did in theirs!

Now when God is conceived as a Lord or Ruler, man is not called a "child" of God. Rather he is an attendant or "servant." Thus throughout the Old Testament men are conceived as servants of the great Ruler. "O Lord, have mercy upon us, thy servants," is an Israelite's typical prayer. "Praise ye the Lord; praise, O ye servants of the Lord" (Ps. 113:1) is the exulting exclamation of the psalmist. "Behold, as the eyes of the servants look unto the hand of their masters, ... so our eyes look unto the Lord our God . . . ." (Ps. 123:2). God, the Lord; man, the servant—this is the basic motif behind the terminology of Israelite religion.

What should be the distinctive attitude of a man toward God? A modern Christian would answer immediately: A man should "love" the Lord, for this is the first commandment of Jesus. Taking the Old Testament a a whole, the most distinctive attitude of a man toward his Ruler, we are informed, is one of "fear." Say the Psalmists: "The fear of the Lord is the beginning of wisdom" (111:10); "serve the Lord in fear"

[1] For an elaboration of this point see the writer's article, "The Terminology of Old Testament Religion and Its Significance," *Journal of Near Eastern Studies*, I (1942), 404 ff.

(2:11); "in thy fear will I worship" (5:7); "the fear of the Lord is clean, enduring forever" (19:9).

Now this word "fear" has often been misunderstood and caricatured. It does not refer primarily to a groveling attitude before a terrible and unpredictable Being. It rather calls attention to the fact that God is God and man is man and that man should show proper deference toward his Maker and Ruler. While "fear" is the basic meaning of the Hebrew word, in common usage it came to designate little more than "reverence." The Old Testament reiterates constantly that a man is a fool, an ignorant, silly person, if he does not show proper reverence to, deference toward, or "fear" of, the great, transcendent Being who has created him and determined his destiny and who rules the times and the seasons of his history and nature. God is the sovereign Lord, it repeats. If you call him a Father, honor him! If you call him a Master, "fear" him! (Mal. 1:6). Without that attitude of reverence and humility, there is no such thing as true religion, for you lack the true knowledge of God. You are attempting to place yourselves on a level with God, so that you need no longer be dependent on him! The Old Testament writers in emphasizing this point throw an unfavorable light upon a section of religious thinking today, unfortunately far too large. This group has minimized the fearfulness of God's righteous judgment on human sin until the urgency of the gospel has been diluted to such statements as: Be as good as you can, and give your neighbor a fair deal! This injunction is valid; but the Old Testament is pointing to an emphasis, an attitude, and an urgency which puts fire behind such watered versions of the Golden Rule.

The phrase "fear of the Lord" was so familiar and so frequently used by Israelites that it became a synonym of "worship," at times even a synonym of our word "religion." Following the Ruler-servant motif, we find that the phrase "to be religious" in the Old Testament is expressed, as we should expect, by the two Hebrew words "to serve" and "to hear, hearken, be obedient." If God is sovereign Lord, then the servants must "serve" and "be obedient." "To obey is better than to sacrifice, and to be attentive than the fat of rams," Samuel is reported to have exclaimed to Saul (I Sam. 15:22). If the servants will not obey, then they are sinners, for a sinner is one who is disobedient and rebellious. God is Lord, said the prophets; let a man rebel or refuse to obey him at his peril.

But what is it that a man must obey? The term in the Old Testament which can most nearly be compared with our theological word "revelation" is "glory." The root meaning of the Hebrew word of which this is the translation is "to be heavy." In secular usage a man's "glory" was that about him which was weighty or important. God's "glory" originally referred to the imposing nature of his appearance. Israelites believed that it is impossible for a man really to see God. What one sees is God's "glory," a shining, refulgent envelope which surrounds his being. Thus we hear of the pillar of cloud and of fire in the Wilderness, of the cloud at the dedication of Solomon's temple, and in the visions of Isaiah and Ezekiel (I Kings 8:10–11; Isa. 6:4; Ezek. 1:26 ff.). This cloud was not God; it concealed God and was his "glory." And from this point it was but a logical step for the prophets to extend the meaning of the word to include the whole of God's self-revelation in nature and in history. In his vision Isaiah heard the seraphim singing: "Holy, holy, holy is the Lord of hosts; *the whole earth is full of his glory*" (6:3). "*The heavens declare the glory of God, and the firmament showeth his handiwork*," exclaims a psalmist (19:1). "Glory" in such passages has become the inclusive term for all evidences of God's being and revelation which can be seen anywhere.

For the ordinary Israelite, however, the most important part of God's revelation is the *Law*. The "glory" of God seems to refer primarily to God's activity and revelation of himself. The Law is the revelation of God's will for man. It is exceedingly important, for it is the Divine constitution for the regulation of society. Man's duty is to obey it; and if he does not, he rebels against God. In keeping with the Ruler-servant picture, it was believed that the Ruler had given to his servants his statutes and ordinances or commands—a constitution which they must keep.

But what is the precise content of the Law? On this point there was disagreement among the religious leaders of Israel, at least after the ninth century. The priests made their living by serving as intermediaries between God and man, showing the latter how best to order his services of worship. In the course of time elaborate regulations came into being, informing priests and people as to just how they could be cleansed of uncleanness, sacrifice properly, etc. Even these elaborations were thought by the priestly group to go back to the days at Sinai, when they had been given by God to Moses. It was natural, therefore, for this party to conceive of God's law as *primarily* a ritualistic law. Why does suffering fall upon us? Because, they said, we have been ceremonially unclean; because we have not had enough services of worship, ordered them properly, or taken part in them sincerely or sufficiently.

Among the prophets there were those who had little patience with this emphasis. Said Amos: "I hate, I despise your feasts (saith the Lord); and I will smell no savor at your solemn assemblies. Though you offer me burnt offerings . . . . I will not accept them. . . . . But let justice roll down as waters and righteousness as a mighty stream" (5:21 ff.). Said Hosea: "For *hesed* ["faithfulness to the obligations of the covenant"] I desire, not sacrifice, and knowledge of God more than burnt offerings," saith the Lord (6:6). Micah gave his classic definition of true religion in this connection (6:6 ff.). How shall a man worship? said he. Shall he come before the Lord with burnt offerings and yearlings and thousands of rams and rivers of oil? Certainly not! God "hath showed thee, O man, what is good. And what doth the Lord require of thee but to do justly, to love faithfulness [*hesed*], and to walk humbly with thy God!"

Other prophets and prophetic writings speak in the same vein. The Fifty-first Psalm is an excellent illustration of the conflict of opinion. The first seventeen verses were written from the prophetic point of view, concluding with these familiar words: "For thou desirest not sacrifice; else would I give it. Thou delightest not in burnt offering. The sacrifices of God are a broken spirit; a broken and a contrite heart, O God, thou wilt not despise." Now what were the priests, who were to use this psalm in their worship, going to do with these words? They undoubtedly agreed with their intention, but the emphasis was too outspokenly antiritual. After the Exile, the old ways of thinking and worshiping had reasserted themselves even more strongly. The priestly viewpoint had triumphed, and prophets like Amos, Hosea, Isaiah, and Jeremiah were no longer to be heard. It was inconceivable in that day, therefore, that God was not entirely pleased with the elaborate ritual. Was not the ritual ordained in the law of Moses? they asked. To guard the people against taking the "wrong" idea from the psalm two verses were added to it: "Do good in thy good pleasure unto Zion; build thou the walls of Jerusalem.

Then shalt thou be pleased with the sacrifices of righteousness, with burnt offering and whole burnt offering. Then shall they offer bullocks upon thine altar." In other words, these two verses are telling the reader that as soon as he gets busy and helps build the ruined walls of Jerusalem, then all will be well and God will again be pleased with burnt offerings!

Walking humbly before the Lord, hating evil and loving good (Amos 5:15), *was the essence of the Law according to the prophets.* Amos and Jeremiah even went so far as to deny entirely that God gave any command concerning ritual to Moses and the people at Sinai: "Thus saith the Lord of hosts . . . . I spake not unto your fathers, nor commanded them in the day that I brought them out of the land of Egypt, concerning burnt offerings or sacrifices. But *this* thing I commanded them saying: Obey my voice, and I will be your God, and ye shall be my people . . . . " (Jer. 7:21 ff.). "Sacrifices and offerings did ye bring to me in the wilderness forty years, O House of Israel!" (Amos 5:25).

Of course, this difference between the prophetic and the priestly attitude with regard to the essential content of the law can be exaggerated out of due proportion. If the prophets had had the opportunity to set up the type of worship which they desired, it is to be doubted whether they would have abolished the sacrificial system of worship entirely. The difference is one of emphasis. Those of us who are engaged in the work of keeping a religious organization together are continually in danger of seeing only the trees and not the forest. Many in the various branches of the Christian church today continue their work as typical priests, laying emphasis upon certain types of organization, certain prescribed forms, claimed to be Apostolic or more in keeping with the spirit of Jesus or of the early church— just as the Israelite priests claimed their forms to be Mosaic.

The prophetic mind continually calls attention to the laws of eternal right, to God, his being and his will, and to the proper attitude which man must have toward him. From such a perspective the exact forms of worship and of organization are of secondary importance. The attitude of Jesus on this point is exactly that of the prophets: "The Sabbath was made for man, not man for the Sabbath" (Mark 2:27). "Not everyone that saith unto me, Lord, Lord, shall enter into the kingdom of heaven, but he that doeth the will of my Father which is in heaven" (Matt. 7:21). Before the ecumenical movement in the world today can go very far, its leaders must convert many more to the prophetic point of view.

According to the religion of Israel, then, it was imperative that a man be obedient to the law of God, just as a servant must obey the commands of his master or ruler. But how is he to learn about this law? It is to be learned from God's *messengers*, the lawgivers and the prophets. The very word "prophet" in the Hebrew refers to the nature of the prophet's mission. That mission is not primarily to reveal the hidden mysteries of the future, as many interpret it today. It is to be God's messenger or spokesman to the people. This we know not merely from the etymology of the Hebrew word (which seems to refer to one's being called as a spokesman) but also because the term "messenger" was actually applied to the prophets in Exilic and post-Exilic times. Even before the Exile, Isaiah thought of himself as *one sent by God* to the people (6:8), and all the prophets began their preaching with the words: "Thus saith the Lord"—the words of a messenger or spokesman of the Ruler. Here again we observe the ubiquity of the Master-servant motif in the Old Testament religious thinking. The prophet's consciousness of having a definite commission from the Creator and Ruler of all things gave a supreme urgency and compulsion to his preaching. In this connection we recall the desperate complaint of Jeremiah (20:7 ff.). He continually spoke about violence and destruction until people laughed at him. But when he decided to speak no more of the Word of the Lord, "then it was in my heart like a burning fire shut up in my bones. I am weary of holding it in; I cannot endure it!"

One interesting question which arises in this connection is: How can one distinguish between a true and a false prophet? In both the Old and the New Testaments there is a great deal of denunciation of false prophets. They appear to have been a special problem to Jeremiah and Ezekiel, who devoted sections of their prophecy to them (cf. Jer. 23:9 ff. and Ezek. 13:1 ff.). They are charged with superficial optimism which the people love, with immoral teaching and living, with lack of originality and inner conviction, and with unfaithfulness to the Divine revelation. The great prophets seemed to believe that the validity of their message should be obvious to anyone who had proper knowledge of the Lord. The Word of God was its own witness and needed only to be made real to the people through the events of the past. We are reminded here of the similar position of the Reformers, outlined in our first chapter. God's truth need not be substantiated by devious argument. It need only be *proclaimed;* and if people will not hearken, it is because of dulness, insensitivity, and rebellion in their hearts. If they doubt this to be God's Word, let them try to stand on the side lines and watch the outcome at their own peril. In the last analysis history must and will be the judge (Jer. 28:8 f.).

There is a lesson here for our own day. Many of us have been doing more reasoning and arguing than *proclaiming* the word of the Lord. Argument is valid, and theological dissertations are a necessity. But here again we come to a matter of emphasis. If the truth of God the King is to produce convic-

tion, to strike at the will, to reorganize life, it must above all
be preached and proclaimed, lest we lose ourselves in discussion and fail to utter it at all! It is at this point that the biblical
study of the last century failed us. Its methods and argument
were basically valid, but its proclamation of the saving faith
was diluted in the waters of overconfident rationalism.

Thus we have seen that the Ruler-servant picture is at the
root of the religious terminology of the Old Testament. Other
key words and conceptions will be discussed in the chapters to
follow, but we should pause here for a few remarks about the
validity of this picture. The great value of the Father-son conception has been pointed out clearly by Jesus in the Parable of
the Prodigal Son. But that does not justify the popular homi-
letical custom of contrasting Jesus' Father with the more fear-
inspiring Ruler of the Old Testament, to the detriment of the
latter. We should remember that both are purely anthropomorphic terms, attempts to make more real to man the essential nature of God. And with both we can fall into error. The
Father-son picture is in continual danger of degenerating into
sentimentality. How often this has happened in the past and
present generations! It is time we should refuse to put up with
the orgies of sentiment that have surrounded much of our talk
of God, especially with the frequent use of "endearing "epi-
thets! God, after all, is God; and man, to be religious at all,
must at least know his place and feel a proper reverence in the
presence of the great Creator and Ruler of all. In this modern
age the father's place in the family is no longer what it used
to be! In our thinking about God a similar change has oc-
curred, until, with our popular creed of the fatherhood of God,
the sonship and the brotherhood of man, the leadership of
Jesus, salvation by character, and the inevitable progress of
mankind, we have persuaded ourselves that this is a lovely

world with nothing at all to fear. God?—he is a wonderful Father, almost too good to deny us anything and far too polite to punish us for misdeeds!

The Ruler-servant picture, however, has likewise been misused. God has sometimes been conceived as such a harsh, cruel Being, so temperamental and unpredictable, that poor insignificant man can only grovel before him. While this is not the Old Testament conception of God, as we shall have occasion to point out in the next chapter, it represents a perversion which is occasionally to be observed. It is necessary for us to keep the essential values of both pictures before us, just as Jesus so frequently did: "I thank thee, O Father, *Lord* of heaven and earth" (Matt. 11:25). "Our Father who art in heaven, *hallowed* be thy name, thy *Kingdom* come. . . . ." The conception of God as a Father needs to be united with that of God as sovereign Lord to give it backbone and strength. The Israelite belief in God the Ruler, attention to whose law is a matter of life and death, is the very ground and source of the Christian belief in the necessity of obedience to the Divine will.

CHAPTER IV

"FOR I AM THY GOD": THE LIVING AND ANTHROPOMORPHIC GOD

Not long ago, while discussing with a group of men such institutions as the Young Men's and Young Women's Christian Associations, I attempted to point out that there are many who are trying to make the humanitarianism of such institutions an end, a religion in itself. It is impossible for this attempt to succeed, I argued, since the brotherhood ideal in our Western culture is a by-product of the Judeo-Christian search for God and his will for man. One of the men, a secretary of the Young Men's Christian Association, was convinced of the truth of this argument; "but," said he, "what is God? There appear to be many gods among the peoples of the earth. I was taught in college that God is the sum of our human ideals. Is that what he is?"

This remark illustrates one of the central problems facing our religious world—the problem of the nature of God. How can we believe in the biblical conception of the personal, living Lord, the Ruler of nature and history, the God who is continually and energetically revealing unto man his creative will, when we live in a world of natural law and think in terms of modern science? The old conflict between science and biblical religion is far from resolved in our modern minds. How can we give thanks to God for our food, when we buy it from a market, which in turn got it from a jobber, who got it from factories and farms, which got it from the land by sowing, cultivating, and reaping. Of course, we can observe the principle of order in the universe. But, while our minds can comprehend a principle, they are scarcely moved to give thanks to it! The God of biblical faith, who was conceived as a person and described in human terms, is not easy for the modern mind to accept. We ask: Is God outside the world, in it, a part of it, a principle, an ideal, or what? Who is he? What is he? Where is he? These questions find no ready answer in the religious world. The simple fact is that, since the advent of modern science, it is difficult for us to say much about the *being* and nature of God.

Faced with this problem, the German theologian, Schleiermacher (1768–1834), defined religion as "primarily a quality of life, a 'feeling' . . . . ," "the consciousness of being absolutely dependent, or, which is the same thing, of being in relation to God." But what of the being of God? Of this he has less to say: "God is immanent in the human soul as it rises into perfect self-consciousness"; he is the "universal fountain of life." But that is about all, for Schleiermacher did not believe that God could really be objectively given or described. The important thing in religion is experience or "feeling."

This point of view has had a tremendous influence. There is a great deal of emphasis today in the Christian world upon mysticism of varying shades. There is little said about the nature of God; rather the emphasis is upon religious "experience." The writer was so indoctrinated with this point of view in his younger years that even now he does not feel that he has really worshiped unless his emotions have been stirred up and his eyes become watery. God, in such an experience, is an indescribable Something, a great Blur, hazily perceived through dripping eyelids, the experience of whom, nevertheless, causes one to feel deeply. But to feel what? That is something which cannot be described.

A consequence of this point of view is the great emphasis today on "worship" services. To quote from a recent book:

Thousands flock to "worship services" in which they neither confess their sins nor fear Divine punishment, neither repent nor pray for forgiveness. Unaware of any radical insufficiency in themselves, equipped with a wish that they be a little better and happier, they seek in the "communion of saints" a painless stimulation towards some sort of pleasant spirituality and revindicate themselves in their own eyes and in the midst of a like-minded people. Thus they seek to arouse their emotions and to receive added power to be good and to do good, within well-defined limits dictated by common sense. . . . . *We* want to *feel religious.* We want a technique of worship which will give us spiritual experience without disturbing our minds or our consciences too much. We are now trying to work out set prayers, chanted responses and the like which, once one gets used to them, are inspiring without making undue demands upon one's credulity and thinking faculty. . . . . The whole thing keeps one from falling asleep, and sometimes gives one a feeling of mystic drowsiness. It is restful and pleasant, and rather different from going to the movies. It gives one a sort of "spiritual uplift," and makes one wonder if there be not something behind it. . . . . "Worship" without fear or faith is the ultimate symptom of Protestant degeneracy. When men come to church neither to confess their sins nor to hear God's Word of judgment and mercy, neither to hear God's Law nor to hear of His grace in Christ Jesus, neither to voice the cry of this body of sin and death nor to declare their hope by faith in Him who raised Jesus from the dead, in short when they come to church without their sin and go without forgiveness,—they turn worship into vanity, and religion into a spiritual farce.[1]

This, of course, is and was meant to be a caricature. We could do today with a great deal more planning for decency, order, good music, and the like in our services of worship. The point is that "feeling" or emotional experience is not *necessarily* worship, and we cannot evade the basic question as to the being and nature of God by placing all our emphasis on experience. The word "mysticism" in its proper and historical meaning attempts to do just this. While students of religion have never been able to formulate a comprehensive definition of the term, the features which are absolutely fundamental to it are the introspective nature of its piety and the immanence of its God. The mystic seeks God first of all within himself. He cannot describe God clearly, for God is ineffable and indescribable. The great aim of religion is to have an "inner light" which will give one an immediate apprehension of God in the soul. The way of man to God is from within, not from without. The *word* of revelation becomes little more than a stimulus to spiritual experience, not a direct revelation of God to man. Historical facts are of little importance in themselves, except as symbols for aiding or stimulating the religious consciousness. The birth of Jesus in Bethlehem becomes the birth of Christ within the soul. The holy city of Jerusalem becomes the holy city of communion within.

[1] Joseph Haroutunian, *Wisdom and Folly in Religion* (New York: Charles Scribner's Sons, 1940), pp. 27 ff.

We must contrast this point of view with that of the great prophets of Israel. Revelation, as they conceived it, is no inward experience; it is the Word of the external, transcendent God. And the chief source of their knowledge of God was not from introspection, but from the outer world, which furnishes the knowledge of his acts and is witness to his ruling power. They paid most of their attention, not to a worship experience, but to nature and to history, behind which stands the absolutely free will of the Lord. We never hear them emphasizing the God within man, or a special place in the soul where the Divine light accumulates, or a special human faculty in touch with a divine essence. Furthermore, they believed that the God of Israel is intolerant; he is a zealous, jealous Being, who is forever set against idolatry and sin. But the mystic's God is tolerant, for he is recognized primarily through an experience of peace and beatification.

The greatest difference between the emphasis of the prophets and that of the mystics lies in the conception of God. The prophet's God is not merely an ineffable and indescribable Something. He is much more, for his revelation in nature and history bears witness to a personality which can definitely and clearly be described. The mystic lays most of his emphasis on the inner feeling; the prophet speaks continually about the external Lord. The mystic thinks in terms of union, wherein the "Thou" becomes "I" and "I" becomes "Thou." But the prophet is definitely and unequivocally dualistic, for there is always the contrast and the polarity between "Thou" and "I." To the prophet, man is made like God and is related to God; but God cannot be recognized primarily through an experience of peace and beatification. The Ruler of this world is not immanent or inside of man. Only his will and revelation are immanent.

It might be asked, however, whether the classical prophets did not believe in a religious experience at all. What did they mean by "Thus saith the Lord"? What of their great conversions? Are these not evidence of mysticism? Now, of course, we must allow for the direct working of the spirit of God in the soul of man, and certainly the prophets are excellent illustrations of the power of that spirit. It is one thing, however, to be conscious of the inner as well as the external working of God; it is quite another thing to lay one's emphasis on experiencing God as though he were entirely given within, or as though he were, first of all, to be perceived within. The prophets never emphasize their great emotional experiences or claim them as normative for all men. The experience or feeling itself is not religion but a psychological exaltation under the impress of a great conviction. To the mystic and to many in charge of our worship programs today the experience of ecstasy is the culmination of religion. To the prophet it was only an item accompanying his call. To him religion was concerned with God and his revealed will and, consequently, also with sin and judgment, obedience and faith, repentance and salvation— not primarily with introspective search for an *inner* light or an *inner* "experience" of the indescribably ineffable.[2]

Still another consequence of our hesitation to speak about the nature of God is a tendency toward the exclusive emphasis upon good works. On the cover of a recently published book

[2] In this section the writer has been aided by J. Lindblom, "Die Religion der Propheten und die Mystik," *Zeitschrift für die Alttestamentliche Wissenschaft*, 1939, pp. 65 ff. I am aware that the remarks here may be open to misunderstanding, since the term "mysticism" is sometimes used so loosely as to describe the religious activity of almost any worshiper. In theology, however, if the term has any meaning at all, it must surely be more than a name for any spiritual activity whatsoever. If that is all it signifies, then it cannot be used in serious discussion except in a very indefinite way. If, on the other hand, we are to continue to use it, then the above description of its intrinsic nature is, I believe, justified.

are these words: "This book helps one to live a real Christian life. It has in it a maximum of religion and a minimum of theology." To be sure, good works are essential in any truly religious life, but the word "theology" means "the study of God." According to the religion of Israel there can be no such thing as true religion with a "minimum" of study about the character of the Divine. "My people are destroyed for lack of knowledge [of God]," cried Hosea (4:6). "Hear the word of the Lord, Ye children of Israel," he exclaimed; "for the Lord hath a controversy with the inhabitants of the land, because there is no truth, nor goodness, nor knowledge of God in the land" (4:1). According to the biblical view, there can be no enthusiasm or dynamic for doing good without first of all having an overwhelming conviction and understanding of the will and being of God. "Of course!" we exclaim. "That is obvious." Yet the nature of our emphasis belies any real sympathy for the prophetic viewpoint.

Yet another evidence of our difficulty in connection with the being of God today is shown by the attempts to describe him in such terms as science will permit and in no other terms. God is the principle of integration or concretion; he is the vital urge or energy in the evolutionary process; he is the product of human aspirations, the sum of human ideals. Many who speak in terms like the one mentioned last prefer the "God-idea" to God. At least, this hyphenated word is quite popular. Many more of us think of God as the "That Which" created and established the order of the world. Just as there are physical laws, so also there are moral laws, and we must order our lines by them. This is a moral universe; in the long run it *is* well with the good, and ill with the wicked (so says the historian Froude). God is one who started things going, but no longer intervenes. For all practical purposes he is an "absentee landlord"! Most of us today who are trying to be good Christian theists, believing in the living, intervening, personal God, nevertheless actually live as though we were deists, really believing that God will not enter the details of daily life.

In the midst of such modern confusion we turn to the Old Testament and find the simplicity of the Israelite faith refreshing. This writer cannot argue that it be *blindly* accepted, but he does believe that its obvious values are badly needed in our Christian life.

The proposition which is the great gift of Israel to humanity is simply this: *God is.* His existence for the Israelite writer is completely self-evident, always presupposed, and never placed in question. To be sure, the "fool" occasionally says that there is no God (Ps. 14:1; 53:1), but that is a practical atheism of sinners who have no understanding. God's works, and not his existence, are really brought into question here. The prophets and the psalmists assert with complete naïveté that the whole world bears witness to the fact that God is. Rain and wind, thunder and lightning, hail and snow, mountains and hills, the beasts of the field and the fowl of the air—all bear witness of him. Even sin, falling away from God in disobedient rebellion, is a witness to his existence. That existence is no problem to the Israelite.

God is so completely obvious to the Old Testament writer that he is never defined in a few words. The Johannine writings in the New Testament make three attempts at such definition: "God is a spirit" (John 4:24); "God is light" (I John 1:5); and "God is love" (I John 4:8). The Old Testament makes no such attempt. Yet it is clear that he was differentiated from all other gods of antiquity, especially by the fact that he stood *alone*, without sexuality, without wife, and without children. In fact, the Old Testament possesses no word for "goddess." The mythology of polytheism attempts to explain how the world works by stories about the divine beings who are conceived as the personification of the various aspects of the universe. Such myths are almost completely lacking in the official religion of Israel. God's creative action in history, not the stories of the loves and wars of the gods, is alone adequate to explain the operation of the world.

But of more immediate concern to us are certain adjectives used to describe God. We shall mention four which are especially important. The first is that *God is holy*. "Holy, holy, holy is the Lord of hosts," said the seraphim in the vision of Isaiah (6:3). The "Holy One of Israel" is an epithet frequently used as a synonym for the Divine name. Now the Hebrew word for "holy" means "to be separate." It refers to God's transcendence and is one of the primary assertions in the Old Testament about God. The Israelite religious leaders emphasize again and again God's difference, his separation from man. "The Egyptians are men and not God; and their horses are flesh and not spirit. And when the Lord shall stretch out his hand, both the helper will stumble and the one helped will fall," said Isaiah (31:3). "God is not a man that he should lie, or the son of a man that he should repent," were the words placed in the mouth of Balaam (Num. 23:19). "When I consider thy heavens, the work of thy fingers, the moon and the stars which thou hast ordained, What is man that thou art mindful of him? And the son of a man that thou visitest him?" (Ps. 8:3–4.)

We may note the effect of this belief in God's otherness and separation from man in the familiar conversion experience of Isaiah. Overwhelmed by his vision of God's greatness and holiness, he was unable even to look up to God or speak to him. So conscious did he become of his sinfulness and finiteness that he could only moan in despair: "Woe is me, for I am undone! For I am a man of unclean lips and I dwell in the midst of a people of unclean lips!" (Isa. 6:5). Only after he had experienced the miracle of the Divine forgiveness and cleansing did he dare speak directly to God.

We may contrast this typical Old Testament attitude in the presence of Deity with that exhibited by many praying Christians today. The familiarity and presumption of much of our praying is almost sacrilegious. It is *certainly* so from the viewpoint of a prophet. Such a man would cry out to us: "You presumptuous people, who have no proper knowledge of God! Were it not for his gracious mercy, God would punish you until you knew your proper place. How dare you pray lightly and unthinkingly, taking God's forgiveness for granted even when you have no real sense of your sins and do not repent of your disobedience? God is forgiving and merciful, but you have no right to presume on that mercy or to take it for granted until you are actually repentant and seeking forgiveness!"

There is today such a constant mixing of the Divine and the human that it is often difficult clearly to distinguish the two. There is a leveling process, whereby man pulls himself up until he feels himself almost on a plane with God and pulls God down until he becomes like man. But not so in the Old Testament! God is God; and man knows his place before him. Sacred things are not to be dealt with lightly. Man cannot eat of the tree of knowledge and elevate himself to the level of God. Whatever you call God, said Malachi (1:6), watch out for your attitude. If he is a Father, honor him. If he is a Ruler, reverence him. "Unto you that reverence my name shall the sun of righteousness arise with healing in its wings" (4:2).

A second assertion about God in the Old Testament is that

he is righteous. Righteousness to the Israelite mind was no abstract principle or characteristic of an impersonal moral order. It is a definite quality of the Divine personality, standing over all norms and laws as well as in them. God is righteous in that he reveals to men what is right and helps to achieve the right which is due a righteous people. Man is righteous when he keeps God's law, hating evil and loving good, being reverent and attentive to God, being just to the poor and the sojourner. God is righteous because he is the ever living source of good and is ever faithful to the promises which he has made to his covenanted people. Righteousness, therefore, is to be seen in the constant, personal intercourse between God and man in the realm of the will. Man must be righteous because God, first of all, is righteous and demands righteousness of him. Being disobedient to God's righteous will means the breaking-up of the Divine world order and separation from the One who alone is able to save. Yet, because righteousness is an active, ever revealed quality of God's personality, it is always possible for the sinner to change his ways, to reconstruct the bond between him and God, which his unrighteous acts have broken.

We often think today of the moral law as being just as much a part of nature as the law of gravitation, as though it operated in the same impersonal, automatic way. When one turns on the shower accidentally, the water will fall; if one gets wet when he did not intend to, that is unfortunate; one should have been more careful. So it is, we are accustomed to think, with the law of morality. If men are evil, then sooner or later they automatically bring on themselves and others the consequences of their acts, for that is the way the world works. But nothing could be more foreign to the Old Testament point of view. There it is always possible that God will intervene and save man, if not entirely from the consequences of his acts, at least from the tragedy of them. According to prophetic theology, there is always a remnant which God in his mercy preserved from the fires of destruction. In the crises and tragedies of life God is eternally active, bringing good where one would expect only evil. To be sure, God's righteousness was believed to be "a consuming fire" and to be seen in the punishment of evildoers. Yet because of God's righteousness man could hope for salvation when truly repentant. "Punishment" was no end in itself; it was only to bring man to his senses that he might be saved.

This leads us to a third characteristic of God, according to the Old Testament, namely, that *he is gracious.* It is the failure to understand this term that occasions more distortion and misunderstanding of Israelite religion than anything else. Many go through the pages of a biblical concordance, checking the appearance of the word "love" in the Old Testament. Failing to find many examples of it, they make the hasty generalization that the God of Israel was a God of wrath and that one must turn to the New Testament to find the great conception of a God of love. A prominent preacher is reported to have made this amazing statement before a large group of ministers: "Through the Old Testament there stalks a stern, just, and righteous God, a God who can slaughter little children because blood was not smeared on the doorposts of houses. What a God! Imagine it! And then came Jesus with the conception of 'Our Father'!" Of all the misleading, inaccurate, and distorting generalizations this is one of the worst. It contains just the right mixture of truth and error to make it a devil's own brew of falsehoods! And yet it is no isolated instance; it represents a fairly common view among Christians.

Now it is natural that many Israelites, when faced with war

and defeat, should interpret God's grace to mean salvation from their enemies. In the early period of their history especially, when they were struggling desperately for their very existence and when war was occupying their exclusive attention, they thought of their God as, first of all, a God of war. But are we to consider the early days as typical for all Israel? And do *we* dare stand in too severe judgment when multitudes of Christians in the world today are thinking in similar fashion? It is true that many even among the religious leaders of later Israel emphasized God's wrath more than his love. But even Jesus could be exceedingly wrathful and denunciatory when he addressed himself to the same groups as did the prophets: "Woe unto you scribes and Pharisees! Hypocrites! For ye are like unto whited sepulchres, which indeed appear beautiful outwardly, but within are full of dead men's bones and of all uncleanness!" (Matt. 23:27.) We must remember that Jesus addressed most of his message of comfort to the poor and outcast of Jewish society, to the "sinners" for whom there appeared little help in the religion of the law. But, when he turned to the leaders, he spoke like a prophet of the Old Testament. The latter had tremendous sympathy for the poor, the fatherless, the widow, and the orphan, who were being exploited by the upper classes. But his denunciatory preaching was directed not to the poor but primarily to those upper classes who were responsible for the rotten condition of the social and religious life.

Moreover, one cannot learn about the true nature of the God of Israel by the concordance method of study alone. One who understands his Old Testament well does not expect to find the word "love" often applied there to God. After all, "love" is a human term which comes from family relationships. If you speak of God as a Father, then you could talk of the Father's love. But, if you think of God as the sovereign Lord or Ruler, then you would not speak of his "love" but rather of his "grace," his "mercy," his "long-suffering," and faithfulness to his promises and obligations—which is what the Old Testament does constantly: *God is gracious.* "Love" was used occasionally by Israelites from the eighth century B.C. into later times, for example, Hos. 11:1–4: "When Israel was a child, then I [the Lord] loved him . . . . I drew them . . . . with bands of love"; or Jer. 31:3; "The Lord hath appeared of old unto me, saying, Yea I have loved thee with an everlasting love." But this word is no more common than the Father-son motif in the Old Testament.

Now the Hebrew expressions for God's "grace" refer to the bestowal of a kindness for which there can be no claim. It is entirely unmerited, an action always moving from a superior to an inferior. The two anthropomorphic words "grace" and "love," when applied to God, therefore, mean precisely the same thing. They merely arise out of different social backgrounds. To be sure, the writer has heard attempts to establish a difference between the two. One was to the effect that love can move in any direction, while grace can move in only one. This is true; but *God* "loves" precisely as he is "gracious." The movement *from* God can go in one direction only!

The belief in the grace of God, in the continual flow of unmerited kindness to man, can be seen throughout the literature of Israel. It began with the dawn of history and was especially clear in the pity of God for the oppressed Hebrews in Egypt and his deliverance of them from slavery. God's gracious action in history is so constantly affirmed that a stereotyped sentence was used over and over: "God is gracious and merciful, slow to anger, and plenteous in *hesed* ['faithfulness to the covenant']." That sentence is not confined to the later literature alone but appears as early as the prophetic histories of the ninth and eighth centuries (Exod. 34:6–7). The prophets became so denunciatory of the upper classes precisely because of the latter's wilful disregard of God's action. They therefore searched history to show the people the terrible consequences of this disregard, that a more sensitive national conscience might be aroused.

In the expressions "God is righteous" and "God is gracious" we have the Old Testament ways of expressing the Divine immanence. If God is so separated and far off from man as the word "holy" suggests, how can man know of him at all? The Israelite answer is clear. God is transcendent in holiness, but immanent in righteousness and graciousness. God's immanence is ethically, rather than metaphysically, described. God is not man, but in numerous ways out of pure, unmerited kindness he is actively engaged in revealing his will unto man. The word "glory" suggests the Divine immanence in creation, but it is usually less definite and focused, and in its rootage it was more akin to the idea of holiness than to righteousness and grace. Israelite thought did not probe the problem more deeply than this, for it was uninterested as a rule in abstract philosophical problems. God was simply a great Being who stands in and over the world precisely as we stand in and over the world of grasshoppers.

A fourth assertion about God in the Old Testament is that *he is jealous*. The second commandment contains the injunction: "Thou shalt not make unto thee any graven image . . . . for I the Lord thy God am a jealous God." The Hebrew root really contains two ideas: "to be zealous" as well as "to be jealous." In a day when the battle between polytheism and monotheism was at its hottest one would expect to find this conception emphasized. It is the very intolerance of the prophetic leaders which purified and preserved Israel's religion for mankind. If the cosmopolitanism and tolerance of political leaders like Solomon had had their way, Israel would have had little more to offer humanity than the other people around her. She would have had even less, for the Phoenicians, Arameans, Egyptians, and Mesopotamians had been making great progress in the material aspects of civilization, the essentials of which were transferred through the Greeks and the Romans to Western civilization. It was a part of the genius of the prophets that they saw the true role which Israel was meant to play. Israel was a chosen people whose duty it was to be separate, to be "holy," quite different from those around her. The more her indifference to her holiness, the more diluted would her great heritage be.

It was inevitable, therefore, that the religious leaders of Israel should have thought of their great Ruler as zealously intolerant of all perversion. They could not conceive of their living, active, sovereign Creator, who was busily engaged in turning disorder into order, as being anything other than a zealous Being. And if he were zealous, he must also be jealous. For how can one who is deeply concerned with history, who is holy and righteous by his very nature, be tolerant of evil? This is a point we too often forget. Reacting violently against the intolerant zeal without knowledge in the religion of our fathers, we have become so broadminded as to acquiesce with the large as well as the petty evils in our time. We are almost suspicious of zeal, and we have become zealously jealous of our tolerance. Yet no man who actually feels himself and his world to be under the judgment of the Determiner of destiny, who sees his religion as a matter of life and death, a blessing and a curse, can be anything other than zealously jealous for truth and right. If God is God at all, he must certainly be a jealous God!

We must not forget that during the days of Israel the great religious struggle was that between polytheism and monotheism, between a base, magical, licentious superstition especially known in Canaanite religion and the more enlightened, pure, even austere monotheism of Israel. The conflict between Elijah and Jezebel is more than a thrilling tale for the childhood ear; it is the description of one of the most important battles in religious history. Had Jezebel won, it is a question whether Christianity, Judaism, and Mohammedanism, would exist today in their present form. But it lay in the providence of God for Elijah to win, and, while Israelite faith was further refined and purified in that and succeeding crises, never· again did rank polytheism so seriously threaten to emerge triumphant. In an important sense the issues involved were decided once and for all before Elijah's cry: " 'How long are you going to limp between two sides? If Jehovah is God, follow him; if Baal, follow him!' And the people answered him not a word" (I Kings 18:21).

In the face of such a desperate and critical struggle it is small wonder that the God of Israel was a zealously jealous God. It would have been a sad day for us had he been anything else! Indeed, the God of true faith is always jealous in the Israelite sense, and our questioning of this concept today is surely a symptom of our smallness of faith. Polytheism in simplest terms is the personification and worship of natural aspects and forces of our world. If we can control them by one means or another, then we have gained security, power, wealth, or whatever else we wish. The battle against personification (in the form of Baal, god of weather and vegetation, for example) was won; but the struggle against idolatry is the chief business of prophetic religion in every generation. And in this day the idols we worship are unprecedently plentiful and destructive. True, in Western civilization we are too sophisticated as a rule to personify them as gods, and for precisely that reason they are the more insidious. Money, power, luck, sex, death, impinge upon our worshiping spirits as mightily as they ever did in days when they were objectified and given names. In addition, there are many others equally dangerous: nation, church, Republican party, democracy, white man's burden, and so on, *ad infinitum*. Even the concept of God may become an idol when definitely defined and infused with dogma and emotion. Yet the Lord our God is a jealous God, intolerant of our harlotrous play with our petty idols and determined that for our salvation we must worship him and him alone.

So much, then, for the attributes of God in the Old Testament. We must now ask: Just how was God's *being* conceived? Was he thought of as "principle," or energy, or ideal? Would an Israelite ever have spoken of the "God-idea"? The answer to both questions is a most emphatic "No!" God to the Hebrews was a definite person whom they could describe; and with naive simplicity they proceeded to do so. God was conceived as a great Man, the greatest and finest Man conceivable. It was assumed that he has a body. He speaks, hears, calls, sees, walks, makes, even whistles (Isa. 7:18). He has eyes, ears, hands, fingers, arms, feet, countenance, mouth, lips, back (which Moses saw). He has emotions just as do we; he can burn with anger, hate, be joyful, and be zealously jealous. Without apology of any sort Israelites felt perfectly free and unhampered in using such human or anthropomorphic expressions to describe the being of God. Of course, there are different levels of anthropomorphism in the literature, some writers being more naïve about it than others (contrast the first chapter of Genesis with the second, for example). Nevertheless, in spite of this fluctuation in the writings, the picture is substantially uniform.

Now, in most of our books on the religion of Israel this characteristic of the Israelite thought of God is considered as very primitive and as occupying a low position in the evolution of religion. But it should be pointed out clearly and emphasized again and again that just the opposite is the case. We must remember, first of all, the day in which these things were written. Among the polytheistic peoples of the time there was no clear or fixed conception of what deity was like. Gods were represented as men, as animals, as birds, or as fantastic hybrid forms. There was no clear conception of the real order of importance of created beings. Perhaps, after all, the bull or the serpent is more important in the sight of gods than are men! But in the Old Testament there is no doubt about the matter! Man is formed "in the image of God." God does not have *human* form; man has God's form! Man is like God in a way very different from anything in the animal world. He is the highest and greatest created being. Accordingly, a special relationship exists between him and God—a relationship which can exist between God and no other of his creatures, because that is the very nature of man and the way God created him. The old uncertainty in the polytheistic world is cleared away with one stroke and the subsequent development of the Jewish-Christian religion made possible.

There is a second point which we should remember before condemning Israel's anthropomorphism. Her God was no abstract idea or principle. He was a living, active, powerful God. Hence, anthropomorphism in Old Testament religion was the *very reason* for its dynamic and virile character. It is a question, therefore, whether such a view is not even more "advanced" than some modern definitions of God as the principle of integration, the sum of human ideals, or the vital energy regulating and ordering matter. *From the prophetic viewpoint such conceptions run into the same danger as does polytheism: that of abstracting some one particular force or segment of nature and making a God out of it!*

The prophetic belief in the absolute rule of the living, energetic, powerful Lord, whom men were naïvely willing to picture vividly in human terms, was the very source of the crises in Israel's social and national life. We shall deal further with this point below, but we may ask here whether Israelite anthropomorphism is not the true answer to the modern tendency toward deism in practical Christian living. Of course, there are crude extremes of anthropomorphism into which no intelligent man can go. Furthermore, the change in our view of the world which modern science necessitates must also be frankly recognized. The old bibliolatry is gone, and one cannot blindly and credulously accept something merely because it is in the Bible without considering its temporal and eternal validity (cf. chap. i). But this much is certain—the belief in a gracious God, who has been actively revealing himself in history through the eternal Christ or Logos ("Word") has been the saving and driving power of the Christian gospel throughout the centuries. Dilute that belief, and Christianity loses the very dynamic which made it what it is. In addition, we must say that as long as we are human (and there seems small chance of our becoming gods), we must use human categories to describe the Divine Being. There is little in an abstract principle which can stir the emotions or strike at the will. We are forced, therefore, to make use of such concrete terms as may make God appear to be what he is—a living, compelling, sovereign reality.

CHAPTER V

"YE SHALL BE MY PEOPLE": THE COV-ENANTED COMMUNITY

IN THE Old Testament we witness one of those deadly con-
flicts which occur when God struggles to substitute his
own values for man's secondary concerns. All civilized
peoples of the world have traveled by one route or another
from simple, communal, country life to complicated, commercial, city civilization. Sooner or later, nations, whether ancient or modern, Eastern or Western, have been confronted
with the problems of land monopoly, poverty, taxation, and
war. Before these problems all ancient civilizations fell to
pieces, save one—the people of Israel. The latter continued
to live as a spiritual force in spite of political collapse, not because they solved completely the problem of communal justice, but because their ideal was to weld their theology into
their economics, to instil the love and the fear of God into the
human struggle for a livable world.

It is this fact which shaped the fundamental character of
the religion of Israel and gave it a social impulse which was
later transferred to Christianity. The prophetic message was
never content with the formulation of a system of ideas or beliefs, nor was it primarily concerned with the preservation of
some existing political order or with the cultivation of individual piety. Its concern was rather with the creation of a
divinely ruled society—one which acknowledged and obeyed
the revealed will of its Lord. That revealed will was the constitution of Israel's state. Yet, cried the prophets, it has been

violated at every turn. "For the Lord hath a controversy with the inhabitants of the land, because there is no truth, nor faithfulness [*hesed*], nor knowledge of God in the land" (Hos. 4:1). "A noise shall come to the ends of the earth, for the Lord hath a controversy with the nations. He has brought an indictment against all flesh, and the wicked will be given to the sword, saith the Lord" (Jer. 25:31).

When one starts with the prophetic certainty about God and his purpose with man, the crises of society assume profound significance. One of the great scholars of the last century has described the situation in Israel as follows:

Every change in the old national life, every disorder in society or in the state, opened a new religious problem—a new question, that is, as to the reason why Jehovah suffered such evils to befall His people. To the unthinking masses these things were only a proof that Jehovah was temporarily estranged, and did not lead them to doubt that He could be won back to them by greater zeal in acts of external worship which might with advantage be made more effective and splendid by taking hints from their heathen neighbours. But though the sacrifices were redoubled and the feasts thronged with eager worshippers, all this brought no help to Israel. The nation sank continually lower, and Jehovah still stood afar off; to the common judgment He seemed to have forsaken His land.

Under such trials a heathen religion which was capable of no higher hopes than were actually entertained by the mass of the Hebrews would have declined and perished with the fall of the nation. But Jehovah proved Himself a true God by vindicating His sovereignty in the very events that proved fatal to the gods of the Gentiles. Amidst the sceptical politics of the nobles and the thoughtless superstition of the masses He was never without a remnant that read the facts of history in another light, and saw in them the proof, not that Jehovah was powerless or indifferent, but that He was engaged in a great controversy with His people, a controversy that had moral issues unseen to those who knew not Jehovah and neglected the only service in which He was well pleased. When Jehovah seemed furthest off He was in truth nearest to Israel, and the reverses that seemed to prove Him to have forsaken His land were really the strokes of His hand. He desired mercy and not sacrifice, obedience rather than the fat of lambs. While these things were wanting His very love to Israel could only show itself in ever-repeated chastisement, till the sinners were consumed out of His land and His holy will established itself in the hearts of a regenerate people. Jehovah's purpose was supreme over all, and it must prove itself supreme in Israel though the Hebrew state perished in hopeless conflict with it. He who redeemed His nation from Egypt could redeem it from a new captivity; and, if Israel would not learn to know Jehovah in the good land of Canaan, it must once more pass through the desert and enter the door of hope through the valley of tribulation. Such is the prophetic picture of the controversy of Jehovah with His people, the great issues of which are unfolded with increasing clearness in the successive prophetic books.[1]

One of our prominent theologians recently published a book entitled, *Can Christianity Save Civilization?* As one reads this book, it becomes obvious that the title is not quite accurate, because the author frankly admits that much of our present civilization is not worth saving and he tells us that the present responsibility of Christianity is to preserve the best we have achieved and lead in the reconstruction of a new order. The question, then, is not one of "saving," but salvaging, revaluating, and reconstructing. The title of this book, however, points to a great deal of thinking in Christendom today, the burden of which is that our civilization is tottering and it must be bolstered up and saved. I submit that such a conception is scarcely biblical or realistic and hardly in harmony with the attitude of a Christian who sees the panorama of history as the scene of God's activity and his judgments. The present civilization in many of its motives and ideals is not worth the saving, and it certainly is not evidence of Christian sensitivity to indorse it and seek to save it in its present form and spirit.

We never hear one of Israel's great prophets asking such a question as is the title of the above book. The civilization of the Hebrews was as dear to him as our present culture is to us. But the greatest of the prophets knew that there were issues at stake of far greater importance than the mere preservation of a

[1] W. R. Smith, *The Prophets of Israel* (1st ed., 1882), pp. 68–70.

civilization or a status quo. They were no patriots of the ordinary stamp, fighting for nation and culture above all else. They were quite prepared to see the destruction of their society, for they believed that the purposes of God *must* triumph, even though the Hebrew state perished and the people were dragged into exile. "Behold," said a writer in the Book of Isaiah, "the hand of the Lord is not too short to save, nor his ear too dull to hear. But your iniquities have separated you from your God, and your sins have hidden his face from you so that he would not hear. For your hands are defiled with blood, and your fingers with iniquity. Your lips have spoken lies; your tongue utters untruth. . . . . And the Lord saw and was displeased that there was no justice. When he saw that there was no man, when he was astonished that there was none to intercede, then his own arm helped him; his righteousness sustained him. . . . . Garments of vengeance for clothing he put on, and he covered himself with zeal like a cloak" (Isa. 59:1–3, 15–17).

In a sermon preached in 1852 Robertson of Brighton uttered a prophecy which is timeless. He was discussing the various attempts made by the human race to construct itself into a family, the latest of which in his day was world trade. Britain was then in the heyday of its commercial expansion, and British trade, it was thought, would save the world. He said:

We are told that that which chivalry and honour could not do, personal interest *will* do. Trade is to bind men together into one family. When they feel it their *interest* to be one, they will be brothers. Brethren, that which is built on selfishness cannot stand. The system of personal interest must be shivered into atoms. Therefore, we, who have observed the ways of God in the past, are waiting in quiet but awful expectation until He shall confound this system as He has confounded those which have gone before. And it may be effected by convulsions more terrible and more bloody than the world has yet seen. While men are talking of peace, and of the great progress of civilization, there is heard in the distance the noise of armies gathering rank on rank; east and west, north and south, are rolling towards us the crushing thunders of universal war.

These words have been as strikingly fulfilled as were many of the Hebrew prophecies, for, indeed, we stand this day in a world that has been "shivered to atoms." Robertson's point of view toward his world is exactly that of the prophetic writers of the Old Testament. Given a knowledge of God and of his ways in the past, a convulsive crisis in society is certain to occur when a people separate themselves from their righteous Ruler by rebellious wills, lying lips, and unjust hands.

Leading Israelite theologians did not believe that their people were an ordinary people. They were an elected, adopted, or chosen people. They had been selected by God out of the nations of the world for a special religious mission. Their society was a special, extraordinary community with a peculiar and unique character. What is the special feature of Israelite social life which placed it in a category by itself?

The answer to this question is to be found in the Hebrew word *berith*, translated "covenant." This term had an interesting history. In patriarchal and nomadic society covenants or agreements between individuals and groups were the legal arrangements which made peaceful community relations possible. The expression most frequently used in the Old Testament to describe the negotiation of such an agreement was "to cut a *berith*," referring to the sacrificial rites which once initiated it. Two familiar illustrations of covenants between individuals are those between David and Jonathan (I Sam. 18:3; 23:18) and between Jacob and Laban (Gen. 31:44–55). The rite in the latter consisted of the erection of a pillar (E stratum of the narrative) or heap of stones (J stratum), mutual vows, sacrificial offering, and a common meal. The most important feature of the agreement was that "the God of Abraham, and the God of Nahor, the God [or gods] of their father" was (or were) called upon to be a party to it and to see that it was kept. The well-known Mizpah Benediction really means: "May the Lord watch us when we are separated and see to it that each of us is faithful to his part of the agreement." In nomadic society where there was no centralized authority over the various tribes, contracting parties kept their agreements because they feared punishment from a deity or deities who constituted a third contracting party. Covenants thus made were absolutely binding, and so religion was the very basis of society's stability.

In the period of the wandering, conquest, and settlement the several Hebrew tribes were held together through a religious bond or covenant made directly between Jehovah and the people (cf. Exod., chap. 24; and Josh., chap. 24). This covenant was made of the people's own free will. God chose Israel to be his people, and Israel chose him to be their God. A special contractual relationship was therefore felt to exist between the two parties, a relationship carrying with it certain obligations, the keeping of which meant life and blessing, and the failure to keep, death and a curse (Deut. 30:15 ff.). There is no near eastern parallel to this unusual conception of a covenanted society. Agreements between individuals, cemented by a deity, were common. But the Hebrew covenant is something different: a whole people entered into a special legal pact with its God and ordered its common life accordingly. Righteousness in the Old Testament, therefore, is primarily the doing of those things which maintain the covenant, while sin is its transgression, a breach of legal agreement.

The obligations which the covenant imposes on the contracting parties are expressed in various ways. Yet they are summed up in the word *hesed*. English translators, not under-standing the exact connotation of this word, have rendered it in the Authorized and Revised Versions by "lovingkindness," "mercy," "goodness," "kindness," etc. In Old Testament usage, however, this word does not refer primarily to God's love or grace for man but rather to *the behavior which the cove-nant relationship or a blood relationship requires.* No member of the community can do as he pleases. He must be loyal to his covenanted' obligations; that is, he must exercise *hesed*, in-volving obedience to the Divine commandments which are the laws of the community, a proper reverence (fear) for God, and justice and kindness toward his fellow-men. God, on the other hand, will keep his part of the covenant by exercising or "showing" *hesed* toward his people; that is, he will bring help and redemption to them, will be loyal to his promises to them, and will be righteous and merciful (cf. Jer. 9:24, for an ex-ample).

In the background of practically all Israelite writing was the conception of the covenanted community. The prophets, whether by direct statement or by implication, warned the people that by their actions they had broken the covenant and gave this as the reason for the crises of their history. "To thy mouth set the trumpet [to call to war] . . . . , for they [Israel] have transgressed my covenant, and trespassed against my law. To me they shall cry: 'My God, we, Israel, acknowledge thee!' [But] Israel has rejected what is good. An enemy shall pursue him" (Hos. 8:1–3). "Proclaim all these words in the cities of Judah and in the streets of Jerusalem, saying: Hear ye the words of this covenant and do them. For I [the Lord] earnestly protested to your fathers in the day that I brought them up out of the land of Egypt, even unto this day rising early and protesting, saying, 'Obey my voice.' Yet they obeyed not, nor inclined their ear, but walked every one in the stubbornness of their evil heart. Therefore I will bring upon them all the words of this covenant which I commanded them to do but they did them not. . . . . Open rebellion is found among the men of Judah. . . . . They are turned back to the iniquities of their forefathers . . . . and . . . . have broken my covenant which I made with their fathers" (Jer. 11:6–10).

While certain that the judgment of God was upon Israel for her lack of loyalty to the covenanted obligations, the prophets believed so strongly in the Divine grace that they could not believe God would cast the people off forever. Israel had broken her part of the agreement, and God was released, therefore, from all his obligations. And yet out of pure love and gracious mercy, they believed, he would take pity on them and "make a new covenant with the house of Israel and with the house of Judah . . . . and write it in their hearts" (Jer. 31:31 ff.); or he would make "an everlasting covenant" with them and would bless them and multiply them, putting reverence in their hearts that they might no longer depart from him (Ezek. 37:26; Jer. 32:40; Isa. 55:3 and 61:8).

To understand the deeper meaning of the conception of the covenant society it is necessary to understand something of Hebrew psychology. According to Old Testament thought, the greatest curse which can befall a man is that he be alone. Jeremiah in bitter agony complains: "I sat alone because of thy hand, for thou hast filled me with indignation" (15:17). The horror of such a state is vividly described by a psalmist: "I am like a pelican of the wilderness; I am like an owl of the desert. I watch, and am as a sparrow alone upon the house top. Mine enemies reproach me all the day. . . . . For I have eaten ashes like bread and mingled my drink with weeping because of thine indignation and thy wrath. . . . . My days are like a shadow that declineth, and I am withered like grass" (Ps. 102:6 ff.). Hosea describes the real misery of his people by calling them "a wild ass alone by himself" (8:9). These similes indicate the Hebrew's horror of being alone. The natural and normal place of a man is in human society. As bird and wild ass belong in a flock, so human beings belong in a community.

A healthy, happy man is one who lives in wholesome, harmonious relations with his fellows. For this reason the Hebrew word *shalom*, usually translated "peace," is fundamental for our understanding of the Hebrew mind. It refers to the healthy, harmonious, untrammeled, free growth of the soul in conjunction with other souls. The righteousness of man, moreover, must first of all be an inward quality, the presupposition of right action, which makes healthy community life possible. Sin to the Israelite mind is unhealthy and unwholesome. Three commonly used words for it characterize it as failure or missing the mark, as irregular or crooked action, and as transgression or disturbance in a harmonious totality. Sin means the dissolution of the soul; it is a hardness or stiffness which renders one incapable of living peaceably with others. He who makes his heart hard or heavy cannot link himself to others or submit to their rights.

Strife in the community, according to the Israelite, is contrary to the nature of things. It takes place when the order of the community has given way to chaos. When Israelite society collapses, no one is able to trust his neighbor, and one's enemies are "the men of his own house" (Mic. 7:5–6). The prophets and psalmists inform us that the dissolution of the Israelite community is in full progress. "How is the faithful city become a harlot! It was full of justice; righteousness lodged in it, but now murderers" (Isa. 1:21). Jeremiah cannot trust anyone: "For even thy brethren and the house of thy father, even they have dealt treacherously with thee. . . . . Believe them not, though they speak fair words unto thee" (12:6). The psalmists say that men "speak vanity everyone with his neighbor. With flattering lips and with a double heart do they speak" (12:2). "I am forgotten as a dead man out of mind; I am like a broken vessel. For I have heard the slander of many; fear was on every side. While they took counsel together against me, they devised to take away my life" (31:12–13).

With this background, we can understand how natural it was for the word "peace" to be practically a synonym of the word "covenant." "Peace" refers to the state of those who are united in harmonious society; "covenant" refers to the community and all the privileges and obligations which it implies. We are not surprised, therefore, to find the two words used together. "A covenant of peace" is merely a stronger expression for the covenant itself (Ezek. 34:25, 37:26; Isa. 54:10). In the words of a great Danish scholar,

Peace and covenant are thus two expressions of the common life of the souls. All life is common life, and so peace and covenant are really denominations of life itself. One is born of a covenant and into a covenant, and wherever one moves in life, one makes a covenant or acts on the basis of the already existing covenant. If everything that comes under the term of covenant were dissolved, existence would fall to pieces, because no soul can live an isolated life. It not only means that it cannot get along without the assistance of others; it is in direct conflict with its essence to be something apart. It can only exist as a link of a whole, and it cannot work and act without working in connection with other souls and through them. Therefore the annihilation of the covenant would not only be the ruin of society, but the dissolution of each individual soul.[2]

[2] J. Pedersen, *Israel: Its Life and Culture* (London: Oxford University Press, 1926), p. 308. The writer is indebted to this great book for the development of the ideas on Hebrew psychology in this section.

In this Israelite conception of the ideal society we find a more profound insight into the true nature of peace than many of us have in this present civilization. To the Israelite thinker peace meant no mere warless world wherein every man is able to go his selfish way, amassing wealth and eating and drinking as his heart desires. Rather, peace is, first of all, an inner state from which all that is hard and crooked is excluded. A peaceful man gives evidence of an inner harmony which enables him to live harmoniously with others. It is such men who understand what true peace is and keep society from turning into chaos. By shuffling the balance of power this way and that we may be able to avoid for a time the actual outbreak of killing on a national or international scale; but in so doing we can find no ultimate solution to the problem of war (cf. Isa., chap. 31). By providing free access to the world's raw materials for all men we may temporarily alleviate international tension; but this again does not guarantee that we shall have enduring peace. There must first of all be a will to peace within the bond of peace. There must be a sense of our social or corporate totality, together with a willingness to be true to its obligations. Every individual must be conscious of his belonging to family, clan, and tribe (as the Hebrews would put it) and must labor for their peace and welfare. But every group must also be conscious of its belonging to a larger whole; even nations must recognize their responsibility to the community of nations. Families, clans, and tribes are necessary; yet each is but a part of the larger covenanted community.

We should not forget, however, that the ultimate ground of the covenant is in the sovereign will of God. It is he who has initiated the pact, and the people are loyal to the covenant when, and only when, they hearken unto him and obey him in sincerity and in truth. There can be no such thing as a covenant society without a compelling faith in God as our true Ruler, in whose service alone is our perfect freedom and with whom we have made the pact with all its privileges and obligations.

To be sure, Israel as a whole never shared the beliefs of a few individuals in Exilic and post-Exilic days regarding her responsibility to the world of nations. The Jewish community after the Exile turned its eyes inward upon itself and rejected all obligation to groups other than itself. The internationalism of Isaiah, chapters 40–55, and of the Book of Jonah, however, was destined for ultimate triumph.

It has been popular with authors of textbooks on Israelite history and religion to stress the social nature of its ethics and theology and to claim that writers before the seventh century B.C. thought of God as concerned, not with the individual, but with the group as a whole. Individualism appears for the first time, we are told, in the writings of Jeremiah and Ezekiel. This point is often overstressed. One need only read the stories of the Judges, of Samuel and his mother, of David, Elijah, and Elisha, and even of the patriarchs, to realize that before the seventh century the relationship between the individual worshiper and his God was already thought to be very close. This attempt to place the beginning of individualism in the Old Testament during the Exile is always made with the implication that the pre-Exilic collectivism is inferior to post-Exilic individualism. Such an idea could arise only in an age like ours when the true nature of man in his relation to society is forgotten. We shall return to this point in the next chapter. Here we shall point out only that the Hebrew view of the relation of both the individual and the community to their covenant-keeping God transcends our usual contrast between them. To be sure, Ezekiel's chapter 18 does emphasize an individualism, but the occasion of that chapter was the current proverb ("The fathers have eaten sour grapes and the children's teeth are set on edge"), whereby that generation explained its sufferings by putting all blame on the sins of the fathers and not on its own. Ezekiel attacks this cowardly doctrine and claims that every man is responsible for his own actions, that the righteous shall live and the sinner die. Ezekiel, no less than any other prophet, regarded Israel as a divinely organized nation which had turned its back upon God and betrayed its heritage.

In the present generation we are suffering from an individualism gone wild. Our churches by and large are not zealously for *social* reform. They are stagnant with a futile individualism. We even interpret democracy as made up of individuals who have a right to do as they wish without heed or hindrance. The Old Testament ideal of the covenant community should remind us that no man lives in a vacuum; he is created by God for community. He cannot live to himself; he must order his life according to divinely ordained rights and duties. The self-centered individual is inclined to think mainly of himself and his own salvation. But one who stands humbly in the fear of the Lord understands also our corporate responsibility before God. Man must ever be concerned with the ideal society, with the Kingdom on earth, with "the covenant of peace," else he is disobedient to his heavenly vision.

It is unfortunate that the idea of the covenant has so little place in the Christian thinking of our time. We have forgotten that the very titles of the two portions of our Bible are "Old Covenant" and "New Covenant." In the last tragic hours of his life Jesus fastened on Jeremiah's ideal and spoke of "the new covenant in my blood," thus binding himself and the Christian community together and to God. From that day to this when Christian people have celebrated the Lord's Supper, they have reaffirmed their adherence to the covenant bond which unites them to God in "the blood" of Jesus Christ. Our lack of understanding of the true meaning of this aspect of the sacrament is a vivid illustration of our excessive individualism.

In other centuries the covenant idea has played a prominent role in Christian thought. It dominated the Reformation theology and was especially influential among reformed groups in Holland and Scotland and among English Puritans. The Scottish "Covenanters" are well known for the covenants with which they bound both individuals and nation to God. They heartily believed in the cry of one of their martyrs from the scaffold that covenants would surely be Scotland's salvation.

In conclusion, as an English theologian has written:

A revival of the basic idea of the Covenant Theology in the Scriptural sense would be a wholesome ingredient in the religious thought of today, for when we begin to speak, as so many do, of all men indiscriminately as the children of God and therefore as having some natural claim on God's favour, we are in reality relapsing to the religious attitude of the pagan contemporaries of ancient Israel who claimed the protection and favour of their gods as a natural right. All such ideas are utterly foreign to the New Testament, and rightly so because they obscure the grace of God and make His redemption of small account. New Testament teaching is that only they that have the Spirit of God are the sons of God, only to them that receive Him . . . . has He given the right to be sons of God. The vital truth which the Covenant idea safeguards is the truth that salvation comes not by any natural right but by the free gift of divine grace. So thereby the grace of the Redeemer is magnified and His redeemed people are constrained from the heart to sing *Soli Deo Gloria*.[3]

[3] The editor, *Expository Times*, August, 1942, p. 332.

CHAPTER VI

"BEHOLD, THE DAYS COME": THE OUTCOME OF HISTORY

THE genius of Old Testament thought about the ideal society lies in the fact that the crisis of the community has eschatological significance; that is, not only is the crisis evidence of God's judgment on the present, but it also points toward an ultimate Divine order. The prophets infer that, no matter how sincerely some individuals may repent and change their ways, the only hope for them is that God may preserve them for membership in the new order. "Seek ye the Lord, all ye meek of the earth . . . ," cried Zephaniah; "seek righteousness; seek meekness. Perhaps ye may be hidden in the day of the Lord's anger" (2:3). The prophets saw that the present order was so rotten and motheaten that there could be no hope of patching it here and mending it there through human intention and effort. One could only throw himself on the mercy of God and through faith find the fulfilment of his life in a new order, erected by God out of the transformed elements from the present chaos.

Prophetic thought about the future of society revolved about three main conceptions: the Day of the Lord, the remnant, and the messianic age. The prophets before the Exile were sure that they would soon see that great Day which would be "upon every one that is proud and lofty, and upon every one that is lifted up . . . , upon every high tower and upon every fortified wall . . . , and the loftiness of man shall be bowed down, and the haughtiness of men shall be made

82

low; and the Lord alone shall be exalted in that day" (Isa. 2:12 ff.). "That day is a day of wrath, a day of trouble and distress, a day of wasteness and desolation, a day of darkness and gloominess, a day of clouds and thick darkness, a day of the trumpet and alarm against the fortified cities and against the high towers" (Zeph. 1:15 ff.). "Woe unto you that desire the day of the Lord! To what end is it for you? The day of the Lord is darkness and not light" (Amos 5:18).

The last passage indicates, by contrast, the ordinary Israelite's view of the future. Apparently, he believed that the Day of the Lord was to be a glorious day for him and his people, a day which would bring prosperity and triumph over the nation's enemies. The pre-Exilic prophets held exactly the opposite view. Because of the people's sins the Day was to be one of thorough purging for everyone. Yet, after the Babylonian conquest of Judah and the subsequent exile in 587 B.C., the old way of thinking reasserted itself. People of Judah turned again to the idea of a Day of national triumph, when Israelites from all parts of the world were to be gathered together, all earthly blessings bestowed upon them, and leadership among the nations given them. "Arise, shine; for thy light is come, and the glory of the Lord is risen upon thee. For, behold, the darkness shall cover the earth and gross darkness the people; but the Lord shall arise upon thee and his glory shall be seen upon thee. And the Gentiles shall come to thy light and kings to the brightness of thy rising" (Isa. 60:1 ff.). The idea of the Day of the Lord in this passage shades into that of the messianic Kingdom, so that the clear distinction between the two in pre-Exilic times is now lost.

We see here two patterns of thought side by side. Both believe in the ideal age to come, but they differ on the nature of its arrival. According to one, there is to be a Day of judgment

on all people, especially on Israel, when the righteousness of
the Lord as a consuming fire will bring the suffering necessary
for purification. To the other, there is perhaps to be a day of
judgment on other people; but for Israel it is to be a glorious
Day of prosperity. To be sure, some of the post-Exilic prophets would say to this that Israel had suffered in the Exile
"double for all her sins" (Isa. 40:2), but no such defense
could have been given for the Israelites in the time of Amos.
The optimism of the people before the Exile was untempered
by the realistic pessimism of the prophets. They were largely
unconscious of the depths of evil in themselves and their society. Amos was speaking to the wealthier classes of Israel, and
we may assume that their optimism about the immediate as
well as the distant future was not unrelated to their economic
security.

The optimism of the prosperous in every age produces the
illusion that there will be a utopia without judgment. Such
foolishness has been characteristic of America in the twentieth
century, with its phenomenal advance in the material com-
forts of life, its amazed admiration of its own inventive genius,
and its sense of superiority to the other nations of the world.
What could have been more natural for us than to sit back
comfortably and muse about the progress of mankind up to
our own fortunate level, and about the discovery of God within
ourselves and in brotherhood! Thus, in the circles of liberal
religion there has been a tendency to identify the Kingdom of
God with the present order. We have said: "To be sure, this
order is not all that it should be, but it can be patched and
mended; it can be participated in more fully by Christian people; it can really be made to develop, gradually but surely,
into the Kingdom on earth." In some minds this Kingdom
has been so identified with democracy that men have even

spoken of "the Democracy of God." One well-known thinker wrote at the conclusion of the last war: "It fires our hearts with more than a reasoned conviction that democracy is God's will. . . . . Because we are Christians we feel in our national life the uplift of the divine presence." Before that war another prophesied: "People will be living in heaven right here in the Scioto Valley." The values of the Kingdom "have not invaded the life of the community from some remote and supernatural realm; they have grown up within the stream of the experience of Christians." Our education for democracy "should not be such as to encourage the delusive belief in supernatural agencies and dependence upon them, but it should be such as to convince everybody that things can be controlled and moulded by the power of man." Democracy "demands a God with whom men may coöperate, not to whom they must submit." In the democratic state the sovereign "is neither a god nor the surrogate of a god. . . . . The sovereign is just ourselves when we co-öperatively insist upon providing for ourselves what we want." "Translate the evolutionary theories into religious faith, and you have the doctrine of the Kingdom of God." The Kingdom can gradually be brought into being on earth through an evolutionary process, if we co-operate with God in the establishment of brotherhood.[1]

The optimism of this point of view, however, was not shared by the pre-Exilic prophets quoted above, for it lacks an adequate understanding of human sin and of the ways of God in history. The faith of these prophets in the gracious mercy of God was so keen that they were optimistic about the ultimate establishment of the ideal society, but the immediate future

[1] These quotations have been collected by H. Shelton Smith, *Faith and Nurture* (New York: Charles Scribner's Sons, 1941), pp. 33 ff.

for them was invariably dark. If they were speaking in this day, they would point to the present convulsive crisis in history as sure proof that our democratic order is under the judgment of God. They would say to us that the totalitarian states are God's instruments for a purging of our way of life, even though they themselves must fall for their presumption in boasting against him who is their true Lord (cf. Isa. 10:5 ff.). Don't talk so much about co-operating with God, they would say; God is Lord and you can co-operate with him only by submission to his will. The chief end of man is to hearken and to be obedient to the law of his righteous Ruler. The ideal order is not man's order to be achieved by him through co-operation with God; it is God's order, and it is God who will bring it about. Man cannot hope to overcome his finiteness but only to find forgiveness of his sins and to live in the hope of God's mercy. In fact, mankind has betrayed its trust. It can only hope that, after the day of purging, God will renew his promises in an "everlasting covenant." The prophets both before and after the Exile believed in the ideal society, but they did not believe it could be brought into reality by human progress. They knew little about progress. To be sure, there were reforms in the society, notably that under Josiah in 621 B.C.; but, judging from Jeremiah's attitude, the "little better" which may have resulted from that reform was not worthy of being mentioned. History is not a progressive journey toward the Absolute; it is a story of the tragedies of man's waywardness. God must intervene in history in some decisive way, else man has nothing for which to hope.

This picture at first glance would appear to be nothing more than dismal and discouraging. Can man do nothing whatsoever? Has he no freedom in absolute obedience to God other than a freedom to disobey? In answering this question we must ask how it is that the prophets and others like them who have laid such emphasis upon obedience have at the same time been the most religiously creative spirits of our past. Somehow, obedience and freedom and creativity go together, and the first is responsible for the second and third. Obedience in the prophetic sense means committing one's self wholly and completely to the law of God; and that law is given by God for our salvation and for our guidance in dominion and government of the world. Two things, then, can be said. One is that obedience to the spiritual law means liberation from egocentric particularism, from socially destructive hardness of heart, from the "law of sin and death," to the glorious freedom of normal creative fellowship with man and God. The other is that the determination of God's law for the specific issues which face us is no simple matter, and it was not so even for the prophets (cf. the struggles of Jeremiah with God, himself, and the false prophets). The creativity of the prophets lay in their interpretation of the law for the people of their day, and therein they, and we like them, found and can find our true freedom. Yet that freedom and that creativity arose and can arise only in a previous absolute commitment to God and his law. The prophetic view of the current society *was* rather dismal and discouraging; yet it was realistic, for history has proved it right. At the same time, the darkness of that present was suffused in the prophetic mind with a brilliant hope, for these men believed in God and in his purpose of redemption.

It has been pointed out that the doctrines of Karl Marx are in a sense much closer to prophetic thought than the socialism of liberal democrats. Marx taught revolution, a violent crisis in the established order, which he believed would usher in the ideal classless society. Utopia, he said, will be at hand as soon as the lower classes arise and do away with the capitalistic stranglehold upon them. In this view we have the prophetic idea of crisis in history, but it is coupled with a most unprophetic and naïve view of man and of his ability to erect utopia. Apparently, only capitalists are sinners to Marx, while the common people are entirely sinless.

Some conservative Christian groups, notably the premillenarians, have kept a firm hold on the prophetic ideas of human sin, Divine righteousness, and the Day of the Lord. The premillenarian glories in the sinfulness, suffering, and tragedy of the world, because in these he sees the proof that God will soon erect the millennium of peace. He takes the prophecy of the Day of Judgment literally, believes that it has never been fulfilled, and sees every great crisis as evidence that it is at hand. Such thinking is, of course, not unlike Old Testament prophecy. Yet we must face the fact that all the prophets believed that the Day was near their own time. Amos in the eighth century believed it was to come with the Assyrian captivity; Jeremiah in the late seventh and early sixth centuries believed, in all probability, that it was to be brought in by the Babylonians; the author of Isaiah, chapters 40–55, about 540 B.C., was sure that Cyrus the Persian was the Lord's anointed to usher in the new day; and Haggai and Zechariah some twenty years later were equally sure that it would come in their time and that Zerubbabel would be the Messiah. In each case the prophets were both right and wrong. A Day of the Lord was at hand, and yet it did not turn out to be *the* Day that they expected. Are we to conclude from this fact that, since the prophecies were not literally fulfilled then, they are sure to be in our own day or in some future day? It would seem far more legitimate to conclude that the prophets had laid hold on a great truth, though their exact formulation of it in time was limited by their perspective; namely, that in every juncture of history, in every crisis of personal and social life, there is a Day of the Lord. That Day is always present for those who have eyes to see it, and *yet it is ever about to come.* The judgment of God is always upon us, though we become aware of it when we find ourselves in a crisis.

Such a conception of the Day of Judgment is more than a fact to be deduced from history. It is also an assertion of faith in *God*, and not man, as the Lord of history. One who believes in the transcendence of God and in his righteousness as against the stark reality of human sin in all its tragedy, finds the clue to history in God's governing will, issuing in a series of crises because of man's disobedience. The days of judgment are evidence that only God's intervention in wrath and mercy can usher in the ideal society. A man cannot acquiesce and even glory in the world's tragedy as the premillenarian appears to do. He is part of it and responsible for it. He must repent and seek forgiveness, throw himself into the present struggle, and then cast himself in hope and faith on the mercies of God. This is the essential view of the prophets, and it is exactly how they themselves lived in the crises of their time. They show with forceful clarity that the one-sided emphases of both modern liberals and ultra-conservatives are so partially true as to be quite false!

A second fundamental element in the prophetic thought about the future is the doctrine of the remnant. Isaiah named one of his sons "Shear-jashub," meaning "A remnant shall return," thus making him a living symbol of one of the main portions in his message. Faced with the danger of an Assyrian destruction of Judah and Jerusalem in 701–700 B.C., Isaiah comforted his people, saying: "And it shall come to pass in that day that the remnant of Israel and such as are escaped of the house of Jacob, shall no more again stay upon him that smote them, but shall stay upon the Lord, the Holy One of Israel, in truth. The remnant shall return, even the remnant of Jacob, unto the mighty God. For though thy people Israel be as the sand of the sea, yet [only] a remnant shall return. Destruction is decided upon, overflowing with righteousness" (10:20 ff.). "For out of Jerusalem shall go forth a remnant, and they that escape out of mount Zion. The zeal of the Lord of hosts shall do this" (37:32).

This prophecy must have been received with mixed feelings. Isaiah was certain that a group would survive the terrible days to come; yet he was equally certain that judgment and destruction would descend upon them and that *only* a remnant would survive. He saw the remnant as obeying God and leaning upon him "in truth." The word here translated "truth" is often used in conjunction with the word *hesed*, discussed in the last chapter, and is almost a synonym for it. It does not refer to some abstract quality in the universe but rather to a firmness or faithfulness with regard to one's Divine obligations. It was the faith of Isaiah that the remnant would be purified and become the bearer of the new order established by God. Later prophets express this view even more clearly. The remnant is to be a cleansed, transformed group with whom God could enter an everlasting covenant, a new covenant written on the individual's heart.

Thus the prophets seized upon another great verity. In a sense there is a remnant which survives every crisis, one which is transformed and turns to God with greater zeal in repentance and faith. Such a remnant is at all times the true hope of society for a better future. It may be that the Christian church has overemphasized its ideal of inclusiveness at the expense of the ideal of a zealous remnant.

An important question for our time, however, is this: How

does one become a member of the remnant? Is it by repentance and good works? If a man co-operates with God as well
as he can, is he sure to become one of the remnant? Post-
Exilic Judaism would have been inclined to answer this question with an unequivocal "Yes." The returned exiles were
sure that they were the remnant about whom the early
prophets had spoken (Hag. 1:12; Zech. 8:6, 12), and they believed that if they now turned to the Lord with greater zeal
God would establish the "golden age" with them as the prin-
cipal recipients of its benefits. The priestly doctrine of works
had triumphed, though, to be sure, prophetic ideals of justice
were incorporated into the law. The emphasis was now upon
the keeping of the legal prescriptions of Deuteronomy and of
the priestly code which was then being edited or had recently
been published. Consequently, there was an objective standard of judgment as to just who is righteous and who is a sinner.
The righteous man became one who kept the law; the sinner,
one who did not. The righteous was, of course, worthy of
God's salvation and certain to receive it, while the unrighteous
had no merit and would certainly not receive a reward from
God (cf. Ps. 1).

The pre-Exilic prophets were by no means so certain about
who is righteous and who is not. They are sure about unrighteousness and appear to believe that in the sight of God
everyone is unrighteous. Isaiah expressed this view: "Woe is
me . . . . for I am a man of unclean lips and I dwell in the
midst of a people of unclean lips" (6:5). In the book of Jeremiah we read: "The heart is deceitful above all things and
desperately wicked . . . ." (17:9). Even a ninth-century
writer was emphatic on this point: "And the Lord saw that
the wickedness of man was great in the earth and that every
imagination of the thoughts of his heart was only evil contin-

ually. . . . . For the imagination of man's heart is evil from his youth" (Gen. 6:5, 8:21).

Now, with such a point of view, the pre-Exilic prophets could not be sure as to just who was to be a member of the remnant. One must throw himself into the struggle, repent, and seek righteousness, but he is not therefore assured of salvation. It is only God's righteous and merciful zeal which can save a man. "Seek ye the Lord, all ye meek of the earth who have worked for his justice. Seek righteousness; seek meekness. Perhaps ye may be hidden in the day of the Lord's anger" (Zeph. 2:3). We should pay particular attention to the word "perhaps," a word partly obscured in the Authorized and the Revised English translations. "Hate the evil, and love the good, and establish justice in the gate [court of law]. Perhaps the Lord God of hosts will be gracious unto the remnant of Joseph" (Amos.5:15). These are remarkable verses, for they are clearly in direct opposition to the view of the post-Exilic priestly community. No man can assure himself of salvation or of membership in the remnant; only God's mercy will determine that.

This prophetic teaching about the remnant comes from a profound honesty in the understanding of man and is a much-needed antidote to one-sided emphases of the present day. Man's co-operation with God is essential in the religious life. But we may not think of that co-operation so as to consider *ourselves* capable of bringing the Kingdom among us. Only an act of God, saving and transforming us, can bring the ideal order into being. The prophetic point of view is against both the utopianism of the liberal and the pharisaic certainty of the conservative that he will be saved.

Another point to be recognized in the prophetic view is that it overcomes the contrast between the personal and the social gospels. Our minds so easily fall prey to half-truths. On the one hand, there are those who spend their time working for the salvation of individuals, forgetting the social implications of the gospel and the fact that man was made for community. They forget that without fellowship no one can be saved, for life means society while isolation means spiritual death. On the other hand, there are those who forget the individual for the mass, who speak almost exclusively of "society" and the "social order," who appear to believe that man's salvation is to be achieved entirely in social terms. The ordering of the affairs of the mass is the major concern of this group, and it often forgets that, while the individual life is fulfilled in the social process, it nevertheless always transcends that process. The one extreme "would produce discrete individuals who have no interest in society or history," while the other is inclined to "think it possible to offer the individual a satisfactory hope in terms of an ideal society" which is to be created in one way or another here on earth.[2] The prophetic perspective which recognized God as the righteous, sovereign Lord of the people transcends the individualistic and socialistic thinking of our day. These modern emphases are due to preoccupation with man and society first, and with God second. The prophets are always concerned with God in relation to man and men. They knew of no abstractions like "social order" or "society." They spoke the Word of God to individual kings and officials and to certain groups, as well as to the "people," or the "children of Israel," or the "House of Israel," or "Jacob," or "Judah," or "the remnant of Joseph." They believed in the relation of God to the people, but they also believed in the relation of the individual to God. They called on the peo-

[2] Reinhold Niebuhr, *Beyond Tragedy* (New York: Charles Scribner's Sons, 1937), p. 302.

ple to repent, but they knew very well that "society" in the abstract cannot repent. Their God was the Lord of the people, individually, severally, and totally. Hence our modern opposition of the individual to society would have been entirely false to them, and they would have been unable to understand it.

The third point to be considered is the idea of the messianic age. The more severe the suffering and tragedy of the present, the more keen as a rule is the hope for a future life wherein the present crises shall be replaced by perfect happiness. The difficulty with our thought about the future is that what is perfect existence for one may not be so for another. Similarly, in the Old Testament the details of the future hope vary with the writer. One speaks of a righteous king, the Anointed or Messiah of the Lord, who shall sit upon the throne of David and rule, as God's servant, over the righteous remnant. Another writer makes no mention of the Messiah. Still another identifies him with a particular historical person (e.g., Zerubbabel). One thinks in universal terms, believing that God is concerned with the whole world and with Israel's mission among the nations. Another thinks only in terms of Israel and of her future. If the latter speaks about the nations, it is to assert that they will be destroyed or defeated and made subject to Israel. One speaks about the necessity of repentance and a change of heart as a condition of the coming new order. Another says nothing about such inward transformations but concerns himself with the rebuilding of the Temple or with proper tithes and sacrificial animals which shall induce God to establish the new order.

In general, however, all the prophets agreed that the new age would be introduced by a direct intervention of God and that it would be constructed by God out of the transformed elements of the present. The elements which are to be transformed by God include not only the Israelites themselves but also animals, mountains, trees, vegetables—in fact, everything of this earth is to be changed.

The remnant of Israel shall not do iniquity, nor speak lies; neither shall a deceitful tongue be found in their mouth, for they shall feed and lie down and none shall make them afraid [Zeph. 3:13].

Behold, the days come, saith the Lord, that I will make a new covenant with the house of Israel and with the house of Judah . . . . I will put my law in their inward parts, and write it in their hearts, and will be their God and they shall be my people. And they shall teach no more every man his neighbor and every man his brother, saying, Know the Lord; for they shall all know me from the least of them unto the greatest of them, saith the Lord [Jer. 31:31 ff.].

But in the last days it shall come to pass that the mountain of the house of the Lord shall be established in the top of the mountains, and it shall be exalted above the hills, and all people shall flow unto it. . . . . For the law shall go forth from Zion and the word of the Lord from Jerusalem. And he shall judge among many people and rebuke strong nations afar off. And they shall beat their swords into plowshares and their spears into pruning hooks. Nation shall not lift up a sword against nation, neither shall they learn war any more. But they shall sit every man under his vine and under his fig tree, and none shall make him afraid, for the mouth of the Lord of hosts hath spoken it [Mic. 4:1 ff.; cf. also Isa. 2:2 ff.].

The wolf also shall dwell with the lamb, and the leopard shall lie down with the kid, and the calf and the young lion and the fatling together; and a little child shall lead them. And the cow and the bear shall feed; their young ones shall lie down together, and the lion shall eat straw like an ox. And the suckling child shall play on the hole of the asp, and the weaned child shall put his hand on the den of a viper. They shall not hurt nor destroy in all my holy mountain, for the earth shall be full of the knowledge of the Lord, as the waters cover the sea [Isa. 11:6 ff.].

Every valley shall be exalted and every mountain and hill shall be made low, and the crooked shall be made straight and the rough places plain; and the glory of the Lord shall be revealed. . . . . Thy sun shall no more go down, neither shall thy moon withdraw itself, for the Lord shall be thine everlasting light and the days of thy mourning shall be ended. . . . . For behold, I create new heavens and a new earth. And the former shall not be remembered nor come into mind [Isa. 40:3 ff., 60:20, 65:17].

Behold, the days come, saith the Lord, that the plowman shall overtake the reaper, and the treader of grapes him that soweth seed, and the mountains shall drop sweet wine, and all the hills shall melt. And I will bring again the captivity of my people of Israel, and they shall build the waste cities, and inhabit them. And they shall plant vineyards and drink the wine thereof; they shall also make gardens and eat the fruit of them. And I will plant them upon their land, and they shall no more be pulled up out of their land which I have given them. . . . . [Amos 9:13 ff.].

They shall obtain joy and gladness, and sorrow and sighing shall flee away [Isa. 35:10].

And nations shall walk by thy light, and kings by the brightness of thy rising. . . . . The sons also of them that afflicted thee shall come bending unto thee, and all that despised thee shall bow themselves down at the soles of thy feet; and they shall call thee, The City of the Lord, The Zion of the Holy One of Israel [Isa. 60:3, 14].

Now we see from these beautiful pictures of the golden age that the transformation of the whole world order accompanies the transformation of the members of the remnant. In the new order man is to be no disembodied spirit in an unfamiliar surrounding. His life is understood to be so bound up with the natural world and with the people around him that, *of course*, all is to be transformed in the new day. Here again is a complete repudiation of the individualistic and socialistic theories of the present. A man stands before God as an individual, but with him are his fellows, his cities, his fruit trees, his sheep, and the land he lives on. There is no such thing as life without a body, without food, and without family and people. In other words, man is physical, spiritual, and social. Therefore, life in the golden age will include all these elements. It is evident that such a view of the life of the future is much nearer to the Christian conception of the resurrection of the body, which was ultimately derived from it, than to the Greek idea of the immortality of the disembodied soul, which has been so popular in current Christian thought. For the resurrection of the body implies that soul and body are a unity (a basic biblical conception) and also that man must be saved both as an individual and as a member of society.[3]

But how can one believe that all these things are actually coming to pass! The simple truth is that our minds, our reason, cannot conceive just how such things can be brought into being because they can deal only with the present objects of experience. We can *imagine* the sun stopping, the wild animals becoming tame, the mountains and valleys leveled, etc., but our reason cannot conceive how such things *could* happen. The prophets did not attempt to analyze the exact process by which the new age was to come. Above all, they believed in God and in his control of everything in the world. They were sure of his sovereign power and mercy. Therefore, they could not believe that their present society was ultimate, the only one that earth would ever know. And yet they were so convinced of the finiteness and sinfulness of man that they did not see how their order could gradually evolve into anything essentially better. Consequently, while striving with might and main with their present, they threw all their hope upon God. He would intervene, they believed, and transform all things.

This new order which we call "eschatological"—belonging to the last things—is the ultimate one on earth. Yet we cannot form any rational conception of it. Our imagination tries to conceive of future life, and we make liberal use of images. But these images cannot be taken literally. They are symbolic of a truth that transcends the human mind. No man can be certain as to the details of the future order; and the more dogmatic he attempts to be about them, the more he reduces his position to absurdity. The idea of the resurrection of the body, for example, can scarcely be more than a symbol of a deep truth to which a finite mind with a finite language can hardly

[3] See, further, *ibid.*, pp. 287 ff.

give adequate expression. The same must be true of the prophetic pictures of the perfect age. When reading them, one can scarcely escape the conclusion that some of them at least were meant to be symbolic. This, however, does not mean that all of them were, for the prophets were certainly sure of the Divine transformation of all things in the world. Yet for us they remain only partly adequate symbols of the new heaven and the new earth.

For the immediate present, however, the prophetic ideal of the age to come remains as a stimulus and guide in the conflict with the evils of our day. The ideal and the hope are at hand, standing over and above us, judging our weak and inadequate efforts and yet directing and encouraging us to obey God and to live with confidence in his mercy and grace.

POSTSCRIPT

THIS discussion of the central themes of Old Testament religion is by no means complete. There are many areas of the problem of eschatology, for example, which have not been touched. Furthermore, the Old Testament does not possess the last word on the subject. There is, after all, the New Testament, not to mention the literature of the intertestamental period. But these fall outside the scope of our present effort. The attempt here has been to show that the Old Testament indeed presents a revelation and has essential contributions to make to our thinking and life as Christian people. One cannot study the New Testament properly without discovering its deep roots in the Old. The idea of God is not *essentially* different in the two books. The idea of the Kingdom of God as both present and future is to be found in the

Old Testament conceptions of the covenanted community and of the messianic age. The belief in the coming Messiah was to Israel *essentially* what the belief in the second coming of Christ is to Christianity. The uniqueness of the New Testament lies in its presentation of Jesus Christ as the one in whom these teachings of the Old Testament come together into a living and luminous reality.

It is, therefore, quite obvious that a true understanding of the Old Testament is indispensable for a proper realization of the full meaning of the New. It was the Scripture of Jesus and the Apostles. At a very early time the Christian church put it together with the new Christian writings because the two belonged together and were held together by an inner unity. And to those in Christian history who have known their Bibles well there is such a thing as *biblical* religion, the *biblical* mind, the *biblical* attitude, the *biblical* conception of God—implying a basic relatedness which renders the separation into Old and New, while, to be sure, legitimate, of secondary concern. In addition, there is in the Old Testament much material of great value to the Christian life which is not duplicated in the New. The Psalms, Isaiah, Genesis, Job, etc., have always been a great treasury of Christian devotional literature. Furthermore, the preceding pages should show that there are many vital religious themes there treated which in the brief compass of the New Testament are not further developed. In short, the importance of the Old Testament to the Christian church is a perfectly obvious fact to anyone who knows much about it.

Now the average Christian, certainly the average Christian minister, would probably admit the truth of this fact. But the nature of his use of the Old Testament (or rather lack of use of it) indicates that his admission is little more than lip service to an ecclesiastical tradition. The Protestant church during the last century has become increasingly a one-Testament church. To be sure, we read the Psalms in public worship and teach our children about Adam and Abraham, Moses and Elijah. But when we come to the teaching of the real meaning of faith, the nature of God, his purpose and work of redemption, we appear to believe, on the whole, that the people of Israel have little to offer us. Of course, we are Christians, and the person and the Cross of Christ must always remain at the center of our faith. But understanding of the work of God in Christ surely demands a deeper penetration into the *whole* of his eternal Word.

To make the actual situation clearer, attention may be called to a survey recently made of the use of the eighth-century prophets in published sermons from 1914 through 1942.[1] Certainly Amos, Hosea, Isaiah, and Micah present a great core of the central teaching of Israel to the world. Yet, in the 1,845 sermons surveyed, only 74 contained enough material to be used in the analysis. At least 3 of this number were by Jewish rabbis. Fifteen employed a text only, usually lifting it completely from the context and certainly making no real attempt to delve into the heart of prophetic thought. One spoke only of the beautiful style of the prophet Amos and is thus to be disregarded for our purposes here. Giving the rest the benefit of the doubt, only 55 sermons by Christian ministers during the last twenty-nine years, out of a total of 1,845 surveyed, made any basic or illustrative use of the preaching of these great figures of religious history. Of this number, 32 were published during the years 1914–20 and 1939–42. In

[1] Sarah Elizabeth Culbertson, "The Use of the Eighth Century B.C. Prophets in Sermons from 1914 through 1942" (unpublished thesis submitted to the faculty of the Presbyterian College of Christian Education in partial fulfilment of the requirements for the degree of Master of Arts, Chicago, 1943).

other words, the majority came out of periods of international crisis when there was deep searching of heart and remembrance of things neglected.

Now why is it that this situation exists in the church? Why this lack of attention to the Old Testament? Admittedly, we are living in an activist age, in which the Christian's use of portions of Scripture is often influenced by its accessibility— and the discovery of the Old Testament revelation of the Word of God demands time, study, and much concentration. Yet this is but a superficial reason; there must be underlying causes.

To this writer it seems that the major reason for the neglect of the Old Testament lies in the prevailing climate of Christian opinion and activity. Beginning with the "fathers" of modern theology—Schleiermacher and Ritschl—there has been a tendency, expressed or implied, to believe that the Old Testament is irrelevant and unnecessary for the formulation of Christian doctrine. Any fine conceptions that it may have are felt to be so deeply imbedded in a compromising history amid crude actions and assertions that we may dismiss them entirely. This belief misses the really essential point about the biblical revelation: that is, God has made himself known, not primarily in ideas, but in events; and we need scarcely be surprised to find that the people of Israel were sinners and therefore fallible exactly as we are today.

More important, however, is the prevailing fashion of thought in theological circles. This appears in the continued attempt to establish a system of doctrine by employing a philosophical methodology (called "scientific" by the theologians). Beginning with certain axiomatic principles (e.g., the categorical imperative, the principle of order, etc.), we are told that this and this must follow—until we have a veritable hierarchy of ideas, all properly arranged and interwoven. If there is an idea which is difficult to fit into this system, then it is thrown aside as "irrelevant, incompetent, and immaterial." Modern theologians are thus continually searching for and discovering simplified axioms which are understood to be the real essence of this or that. Cogitation reveals that the new essence or essences are the very core of reality; and, if so, such and such must follow. Q.E.D.—our theology is fixed (and fixated)—the matter is closed.[2]

Modern theology is thus no longer biblically grounded. The Bible is used, not as a source for doctrine, but as illustrative of doctrines already derived from other sources or by other means. If there is something in the Bible which does not fit our preconceived patterns, we simply reject it. So it is that our modern theologians are no longer primarily interested in the Bible. *They go to it, not to be taught by it, not to find in it criticism of their religion or of their system, but simply to find illustrations of this point or that.* To be sure, these remarks are something of a caricature; but, nevertheless, the essential character of the average book on Christian theology can thus generally be described.

This methodology on the part of our leading religious minds has created a climate which has influenced us all in our use of the Bible. The average modern minister who makes some attempt to use the Old Testament, for example, is not primarily interested in being criticized, humbled, or taught by its profound insight into the being and activity of God and man. On the contrary, he delves into it to discover clever texts, interesting stories, and good *ideas* beautifully or crypti-

---

[2] For an elaboration of this point see Joseph Haroutunian, *First Essay in Reflective Theology* (inaugural address of the Cyrus H. McCormick Professor of Systematic Theology) (Chicago: McCormick Theological Seminary, 1943).

cally expressed with which he can adorn his sermon. He already *has* a theology; he does not need a new pattern of thought—at least, it never dawns on him that the Old Testament can teach him; and thus he becomes unteachable by it. He is bombarded by lists of texts for the church year, by books on how to use this prophet or that, how to get good ideas or clever notions from this translation or that, and most of all by a variety of tomes from great Christian thinkers of our time by whom the Bible may be reverenced in theory but not in the use thereof. Only a remarkably calm and reflective soul can survive the bombardment and actually penetrate the veil which we have placed between the Old Testament and ourselves!

Yet all the blame for our present situation must not be laid at the door of the theologians. We who are biblical teachers are equally culpable, if not more so! On the one hand, there are those who have never really labored intensively, either in the field of Christian theology or in the linguistic, literary, historical, or archeological problems and background of biblical life and literature. To resort again to caricature, it would appear that in this group the main qualifications for an expositor of the Bible are a normal, consecrated, and intelligent mind, a good personality, and an ability to read! On the other hand, there are the recognized biblical scholars to whom we look for guidance and enlightenment. These men, by and large, are truly learned and sincerely devoted to the cause of truth. They have specialized intensively in the languages of Scripture, in ancient and in biblical history, in literary and textual criticism, and even occasionally in archeology. Their work has been exceedingly important, and yet there has been something wrong with it. Somehow, the typical biblical scholar has been a detached, dissecting technician or historian.

And, as has been pointed out before, such a one can never grasp or explain the deepest meaning of the biblical revelation of God for modern life until he has descended into the arena with the apostle or prophet and is at the same time struggling with the lot of sinning, restless people in our world. Lacking a strong sense of participation in a common search for the will of God in this day, biblical scholarship has been involved with a tremendous mass of details which to the layman have appeared trivial and unimportant.

Now it happens that many of these details, in sum, are not trivial; but the burden of proof has lain with the scholars, and they have never quite burst the bonds of their detachment and triviality. They have been confident and excited about our new understanding and treatment of the Bible, and they have been continually at the point of triumph; but somehow that point has never quite been reached. One reason for this is that they have possessed only a bowing acquaintance with theologians and their work. Individually, they have possessed religious beliefs, but their systems have reflected the prevailing climate of opinion to such an extent that *even they* have approached the Bible, not so much to be taught, criticized, and humbled by it, as to understand it as the great monument of our Christian heritage. This has been true especially of the approach to the Old Testament, where literary criticism and the genetic development of religious ideas have been the primary concern, as though knowing them were the end of the study of the Hebrews, rather than the beginning.

It is a sorry day, then, when the theologian shows no profound interest in the Bible, and when the biblical student pays scant attention to the work of the theologian, and when both treat the Old Testament as a mere monument of antiquity and as no serious revelation of the eternal in the temporal for our salvation here and now. In such an impasse what can we expect from a parish minister or Christian layman!

Yet the situation is not without its brighter aspects. There are premonitions that a new day is about to dawn. Among both biblical scholars and theologians there are those who are becoming increasingly uncomfortable with their former state. We have never been without voices crying in the wilderness, and today they are beginning to be heard. The disuse and misuse of the Old Testament is a matter for concern but not for despair. If, indeed, God has spoken through the history of Israel, then surely his Word will be confirmed in our time or in that of our children. "The same Spirit, who spake by the mouths of the prophets," may indeed penetrate our hearts and convince us, while disturbing the fixity of our fashions of thought.

INDEX

Adam, 21, 100
Allegory, 7 ff.
Amos, 42 ff., 84, 88, 100
Anthropomorphism, 7, 36, 65 ff.
Archeology, 4, 14, 103
Assyrians, 3, 24 ff., 32, 88 f.
Atheism, in Old Testament, 55
Augustine, 8
Authority, of Scripture, 8 ff.

Baal, 64
Babylonians, 24 ff., 83, 88
Balaam, 56

Calvin, John, 8 ff.
Catholic church; see Roman Catholic church
Chosen People; see Election
Christ; see Jesus
Christianity, modern, 17 f., 36, 39 f., 44, 47 ff., 57, 67, 84 f., 100 ff.
Church Fathers, 7
Conscience, 12
Covenant, 22, 72 ff., 90
Crisis (crises), meaning of, 17 ff.
Cross, the, 19, 100
Culbertson, Sarah Elizabeth, 100
Cyrus, 88

David, 23
Day of the Lord, 2, 25, 82 ff.
Deism, 54 f., 67
Democracy, 84 f.
Deuteronomy, 91

Election, of Israel, 26, 63, 72 f.
Elijah, 64, 100
Eschatology, 82 ff., 98
Excavations; see Archeology

Exegesis; see Interpretation
Exile of Judah, 35, 43, 82 ff.
Exodus, meaning of, 22 f.
Ezekiel, 46, 79 f.

Fear of the Lord, 39 f.
Flood, the, 21 f.
Freedom, 86 f.

Genesis, 6, 13, 21 f., 66, 99
Glory, of God, 41 f., 62
God, Old Testament conception of, 19 ff., 28, 36 ff., 48 ff.
Gods, of antiquity, 55 f., 66, 69
Golden Rule, 10, 40
Grace, of God, 21, 59 ff., 75

Haroutunian, Joseph, 30, 51, 102
Hebrews; see Israel, Israelites
Hesed, 43, 61, 69, 74, 90
Hezekiah, 7
History, 4, 16, 21 ff., 89
Holiness, of God, 56 f.
Hosea, 37, 43, 76, 100

Immanence, of God, 62
Individualism, in Israel, 79 ff.
Inspiration, views of, 5 ff.
Interpretation of Scripture, 5 ff.
Isaiah, 1 ff., 5, 9, 12 ff., 25 f., 37, 43, 45, 56 f., 8 ff., 91, 100
Israel, Israelites, 3 f., 14, 55, 84

James, Epistle of, 11
Jealousy, of God, 52, 62 ff.
Jeremiah, 15, 25 ff., 38, 43 f., 46, 75 f., 79 f., 86 f., 88
Jeroboam II, 33
Jesus, 8 ff., 44 f., 47 f., 51, 60, 80 f., 99

107

Jews, Judaism, 5 ff., 11, 79, 91
Jezebel, 64
Job, 99
Jonah, 13 f., 79
Josiah, 32, 86
Jowett, Benjamin, 33
Judah, 25 ff., 83, 89
Judges, the, 23
Judges, Book of, 31

Kingdom of God, 37, 80, 84 f., 99
Kings, Books of, 31 f.

Lachish, 4
Law, laws, 4 ff., 10, 42 ff., 58
Leviticus, 7
Lindblom, J., 53
Literary analysis, 3, 14 f.
Lord, 36 ff.
Love, 36, 39, 59 ff.
Lovingkindness; see *Hesed*
Luther, Martin, 8 ff.

Malachi, 38, 57
Man, 39 ff., 66
Marx, Karl, 87 f.
Messiah, 7, 88, 94, 99
Messianic age, 82, 94 ff., 99
Micah, 3, 43, 100
Minear, Paul, 28
Mizpah Benediction, 73
Moses, 23, 42 ff., 65, 100
Mysticism, 50 ff.
Mythology, 56

New Testament, 36, 98 f.
Niebuhr, Reinhold, 93

Obedience, to God, 41, 48, 86 f.
Old Testament, 5 ff., 16, 19 ff., 68 ff., 79 ff., 98 ff.
Omri, 33
Origin, 7, 9

Peace, Israelite conception of, 76 ff.
Pedersen, J., 77
Polytheism, 39, 55 f., 62 ff., 66, 69
Premillenarians, 88 f.
Priests, 33, 42 ff.
Prophets, 4, 10, 20, 24 ff., 42 ff., 45 f., 52 f., 62, 74 f., 82 ff.; false, 46, 87
Protestant, Protestants, 8 ff., 100
Psychology, Hebrew, 75 ff.

Redemption, 19, 87, 100
Reformers, 9, 46
Remnant, 59, 82, 89 ff.
Revelation, 2 ff., 16, 41 f., 52, 100 f.
Righteousness, Israelite conception of, 58 f.
Ritschl, 101
Robertson of Brighton, 71
Roman Catholic church, 8

Salvation, 58 f., 87, 91 f., 94 ff.
Schleiermacher, 49 f., 101
Scholarship, biblical, 2 ff., 103 f.
Scripture, problem of, 5 ff.
Sin, sinner, 19, 41, 55, 91
Smith, H. Shelton, 85
Smith, W. R., 70
Solomon, 23, 32
Song of Songs, 8
Spirit, Holy, 12 ff.

Ten Commandments, 10
Theology, modern, 101 ff.
Transcendence, of God, 56 f.
Truth, Old Testament word for, 90

Voltaire, 32

Word of God, 1, 3, 6 f., 9 ff., 46, 93, 100 f., 105

Zephaniah, 82
Zerubbabel, 88, 94
Zimri, 33